Richard Peck

WHO WROTE THAT?

LOUISA MAY ALCOTT
JANE AUSTEN
AVI
JUDY BLUME, SECOND EDITION
BETSY BYARS
BEVERLY CLEARY
ROBERT CORMIER
BRUCE COVILLE
ROALD DAHL
CHARLES DICKENS
THEODOR GEISEL
S.E. HINTON
WILL HOBBS
ANTHONY HOROWITZ
STEPHEN KING
MADELEINE L'ENGLE
GAIL CARSON LEVINE
C.S. LEWIS
LOIS LOWRY
ANN M. MARTIN
L.M. MONTGOMERY
PAT MORA
WALTER DEAN MYERS
SCOTT O'DELL
BARBARA PARK
GARY PAULSEN
RICHARD PECK
TAMORA PIERCE
EDGAR ALLAN POE
BEATRIX POTTER
PHILIP PULLMAN
MYTHMAKER: THE STORY OF J.K. ROWLING, SECOND EDITION
MAURICE SENDAK
SHEL SILVERSTEIN
JERRY SPINELLI
R.L. STINE
EDWARD L. STRATEMEYER
E.B. WHITE
LAURA INGALLS WILDER
LAURENCE YEP
JANE YOLEN

WHO WROTE THAT?

Richard Peck

Amy Sickels

Foreword by
Kyle Zimmer

CHELSEA HOUSE
PUBLISHERS
An imprint of Infobase Publishing

Richard Peck

Chelsea House
An imprint of Infobase Publishing
132 West 31st Street
New York NY 10001

Library of Congress Cataloging-in-Publication Data
Sickels, Amy.
Richard Peck / Amy Sickels.
p. cm. — (Who wrote that?)
Includes bibliographical references and index.
ISBN 978-0-7910-9530-0
1. Peck, Richard, 1934—Juvenile literature. 2. Authors, American—20th century—Biography—Juvenile literature. 3. Young adult fiction—Authorship—Juvenile literature. I. Title. II. Series.
PS3566.E2526Z86 2009
813'.54—dc22
[B]
2008035035

Chelsea House books are available at special discounts when purchased in bulk quantities for business, associations, institutions, or sales promotions. Please call our Special Sales Department in New York at (212) 967-8800 or (800) 322-8755.

You can find Chelsea House on the World Wide Web at http://www.chelseahouse.com

Text design by Keith Trego
Cover design by Alicia Post

Printed in the United States of America

Bang EJB 10 9 8 7 6 5 4 3 2 1

This book is printed on acid-free paper.

All links and Web addresses were checked and verified to be correct at the time of publication. Because of the dynamic nature of the Web, some addresses and links may have changed since publication and may no longer be valid.

Table of Contents

FOREWORD BY
KYLE ZIMMER
PRESIDENT, FIRST BOOK

HUMANITY IS POWERED by stories. From our earliest days as thinking beings, we employed every available tool to tell each other stories. We danced, drew pictures on the walls of our caves, spoke, and sang. All of this extraordinary effort was designed to entertain, recount the news of the day, explain natural occurrences—and then gradually to build religious and cultural traditions and establish the common bonds and continuity that eventually formed civilizations. Stories are the most powerful force in the universe; they are the primary element that has distinguished our evolutionary path.

Our love of the story has not diminished with time. Enormous segments of societies are devoted to the art of storytelling. Book sales in the United States alone topped $24 billion in 2006; movie studios spend fortunes to create and promote stories; and the news industry is more pervasive in its presence than ever before.

There is no mystery to our fascination. Great stories are magic. They can introduce us to new cultures, or remind us of the nobility and failures of our own, inspire us to greatness or scare us to death; but above all, stories provide human insight on a level that is unavailable through any other source. In fact, stories connect each of us to the rest of humanity not just in our own time, but also throughout history.

This special magic of books is the greatest treasure that we can hand down from generation to generation. In fact, that spark in a child that comes from books became the motivation for the creation of my organization, First Book, a national literacy program with a simple mission: to provide new books to the most disadvantaged children. At present, First Book has been at work in hundreds of communities for over a decade. Every year children in need receive millions of books through our organization and millions more are provided through dedicated literacy institutions across the United States and around the world. In addition, groups of people dedicate themselves tirelessly to working with children to share reading and stories in every imaginable setting from schools to the streets. Of course, this Herculean effort serves many important goals. Literacy translates to productivity and employability in life and many other valid and even essential elements. But at the heart of this movement are people who love stories, love to read, and want desperately to ensure that no one misses the wonderful possibilities that reading provides.

When thinking about the importance of books, there is an overwhelming urge to cite the literary devotion of great minds. Some have written of the magnitude of the importance of literature. Amy Lowell, an American poet, captured the concept when she said, "Books are more than books. They are the life, the very heart and core of ages past, the reason why men lived and worked and died, the essence and quintessence of their lives." Others have spoken of their personal obsession with books, as in Thomas Jefferson's simple statement: "I live for books." But more compelling, perhaps, is the almost instinctive excitement in children for books and stories.

Throughout my years at First Book, I have heard truly extraordinary stories about the power of books in the lives of children. In one case, a homeless child, who had been bounced from one location to another, later resurfaced—and the only possession that he had fought to keep was the book he was given as part of a First Book distribution months earlier. More recently, I met a child who, upon receiving the book he wanted, flashed a big smile and said, "This is my big chance!" These snapshots reveal the true power of books and stories to give hope and change lives.

As these children grow up and continue to develop their love of reading, they will owe a profound debt to those volunteers who reached out to them—a debt that they may repay by reaching out to spark the next generation of readers. But there is a greater debt owed by all of us—a debt to the storytellers, the authors, who have bound us together, inspired our leaders, fueled our civilizations, and helped us put our children to sleep with their heads full of images and ideas.

WHO WROTE THAT? is a series of books dedicated to introducing us to a few of these incredible individuals. While we have almost always honored stories, we have not uniformly honored storytellers. In fact, some of the most important authors have toiled in complete obscurity throughout their lives or have been openly persecuted for the uncomfortable truths that they have laid before us. When confronted with the magnitude of their written work or perhaps the daily grind of our own, we can forget that writers are people. They struggle through the same daily indignities and dental appointments, and they experience the intense joy and bottomless despair that many of us do. Yet somehow they rise above it all to deliver a powerful thread that connects us all. It is a rare honor to have the opportunity that these books provide to share the lives of these extraordinary people. Enjoy.

President George W. Bush and First Lady Laura Bush pose with author Richard Peck (center) *during the National Endowment for the Arts awards ceremony held at Constitution Hall in Washington, D.C., on April 22, 2002. Peck was the recipient of a National Humanities Medal.*

1

The First Line

RICHARD PECK WROTE his first line of fiction the same day that he quit his teaching job. He was 37 years old.

Peck had been teaching high school and junior high English classes on the Upper East Side of New York City. Though there was much about teaching that he liked, Peck also felt frustrated. This was the late 1960s; the world had changed since he was a boy in rural Illinois. Back then, school did not seem to be so complicated: You went to school and you learned something. Now, the students seemed more worried about impressing their peers than about learning. Peck saw that parents tended to be shifting the responsibility of raising their kids to the schools and that the schools in turn were lowering their expectations.

Peck cared about his students but felt he did not know how to get through to them.

Peck had been seriously considering leaving teaching. He had always wanted to write. Why not take a chance? He would never know unless he tried. Richard Peck taught his last class on May 24, 1971. He went home after seventh period, carried his typewriter into the garden of his Brooklyn Heights apartment, and began his first novel.

Although Peck left the classroom, he did not stop thinking about his students. He still wanted to reach them, but now he had discovered a different way to do so—through his novels. Peck has often said that he never would have become a writer without being a teacher first. His students gave him ideas; from them, he figured out what he wanted to write about. Before embarking on his writing career, he already knew his characters and his audience. He recalled:

> I found those people in my roll book. They were my students, the people I knew best and liked best. Their whims took precedence over my needs, and they had me outnumbered all day long. From our first hours together I knew things about them their parents dared never know. In their writing I read what they dared never say aloud within the hearing of their powerful peers.[1]

HIS FIRST NOVEL

Peck wrote his first novel in about four months. In October, he stacked the manuscript into a small box and hand-delivered it to George Nicholson, editor-in-chief of juvenile books at Holt, Rinehart & Winston. The next day, Peck's phone rang. Nicholson told him to go ahead and start his second novel.

Did you know...

Like Richard Peck, many other well-known, contemporary authors taught high school or middle school before embarking on a writing career:

Frank McCourt, author of the acclaimed *Angela's Ashes*, was a high school teacher in New York City for 30 years; this is the subject of his memoir, *Teacher Man*.

Wally Lamb, bestselling author of *I Know This Much is True* and *She's Come Undone*, taught high school English from 1972 to 1997 in Connecticut.

Frank Conroy, author of *Prince of Tides*, taught in a one-room schoolhouse on Daufuskie Island, South Carolina, an experience he used in writing his novel *The Water is Wide*.

Sandra Cisneros taught high school after her widely read book *The House on Mango Street* was already published.

Tobias Wolff, author of *This Boy's Life*, taught at a Catholic inner city school in San Francisco.

Horror fiction masters Stephen King and Dean Koontz also taught high school. Koontz taught in a remote mining town in the mountains of Appalachia. King taught high school for two years in Maine, and quit after *Carrie* was published.

Peck's first novel was titled *Don't Look and It Won't Hurt.* Although his students were in the back of his mind while he was writing, this first novel was not based on them. He still felt too close to his students, as well as too angry and disappointed with teaching, to write about them in a fair way. Instead, he chose to write something outside of his experience that would be a realistic scenario for young people.

The inspiration for *Don't Look and It Won't Hurt* came from Peck's friends, Dr. Richard Hughes and his wife, Jean Hughes, a couple who ran a local home for unwed mothers in Evanston, Illinois. They provided the young mothers with a pleasant home while they were waiting for their babies to be born. Peck met with many of the girls and felt touched by their stories. He asked the Hugheses what the girls had in common, and they told him that the girls almost always believed they would keep the babies, marry the fathers, and leave home—but that it almost never worked out that way.

Peck thought about the girls and their difficult situations. He felt like he now had the outline of a story and would be able to make up the rest. At first, he tried to write the story from the viewpoint of the unwed mother. He wondered what she would do. Who would she turn to? After several drafts, he changed his mind and decided to tell the story from the viewpoint of one of her younger sisters, Carol, a 15-year-old who tries to hold her family together. The novel takes place in a small town and focuses on a rural family. It is a family of three girls being raised by a single, working mother. The novel explores the relationships between children and their parents, and the relationships between siblings. It also portrays the importance of individual responsibility, one of Peck's favorite themes.

POPULAR AUTHOR

Don't Look and It Won't Hurt sold more than a half-million copies during its first 10 years in print. Following it, Peck

Did you know...

In his memoir *Anonymously Yours*, Richard Peck gives advice "To Aspiring Writers." He writes an explanation with each point. Here is an abbreviated version:

1. Never write what you know. Write what you can find out.
2. Words are the bricks of your writing, and you need a larger supply than you have.
3. Fiction is strongly based on the search for roots. Most stories are family stories. Take time out from avoiding your parents to find out who they are.
4. Fiction is never about ordinary people. For subject matter, look around for the people in your school who aren't full-time conformists.
5. Write each page at least six times. Professional writers are just like students. We never get anything right in the first five tries either.
6. Read a book a week to see how other people do it. Writing is hard enough without the help and inspiration of your fellow writers.
7. Writing requires as much practice as the piano and more than football. Carve out the time from television and spend an hour writing each day.
8. Finally, think of all writing as communication, not self-expression. Nobody in the world wants to read your diary—except your mother.

published *Dreamland Lake* and *Through a Brief Darkness* the next year. He then published *Representing Super Doll.* His fifth book for young adults was the first one in the "Blossom Culp" series, *The Ghost Belonged to Me.* These books put Peck on the map as a successful young adult author. Since the publication of *Don't Look and It Won't Hurt*, Peck has published more than 30 books for young adults. He has published at least one novel every two years.

Peck is a well-respected young adult author, popular with teens, librarians, parents, and critics. In 1988, a survey of 40 officers of the Assembly on Literature for Adolescents of the National Council of Teachers of English voted on the 100 most important authors of novels for teenagers; Peck received more votes than all the others, with the exception of S.E. Hinton and Paul Zindel. For his contribution to young adult literature, he has won the Margaret A. Edwards Award, the National Council of Teachers of English/ALAN Award, and the 1991 Medallion from the University of Southern Mississippi. His novels have been named Best Young Adult Books of the Year by the American Library Association and have been finalists for the Newbery Award and the National Book Award. In 2001, his book *A Year Down Yonder* won the Newbery gold medal.

Richard Peck is tall, energetic, and dignified. His biographer, Donald Gallo, describes him as "a gentleman in the fullest senses of the word: gracious, honorable, independent, and charming."[2] Peck lives in New York City and travels often. He is friendly, candid, and humorous. He is also someone who very much values his privacy.

Peck grew up in a very different time period and setting than the audience for which he is writing—those who live in a world of text messaging, computers, video games, and cable television. Peck was raised by his mother and father in a small, rural town in Illinois. He came from a large extended family and heard many great stories from his elders when he was growing up. He liked to read and went to school dances in high school. He never experienced the threat of drugs or guns in school; he did not feel that there was pressure to wear the right clothes or drive the right kind of car. It was a simpler time.

Peck has, over the years, paid close attention to the youth of the day. He is aware of the many pressures and problems, and he is not afraid to write about what concerns today's teens. Serious subjects that Peck has tackled in his fiction include teen suicide, peer pressure, single parenting, rape, censorship, and death. Not everything he writes is serious, though. He has also written ghost stories, comical novels, and books about cyberspace—despite the fact that Peck himself does not like computers.

How does Peck write from the perspective of a young boy or a teenage girl? He tries to put himself in the shoes of his audience. He wants to understand the troubles that young people face, but he also wants to encourage them to take responsibility for their actions and to reach out to parents, grandparents, and teachers for help and advice. One of Peck's most well-known publications is not a novel or a story, but a poem he wrote that captures how young people feel and what they can do to survive adolescence. This is "A Teenager's Prayer":

> Oh, Supreme Being, and I don't mean me:
>
> Give me the vision to see my parents as human beings because if they aren't, what does that make me?
>
> Give me vocabulary because the more I say you know, the less anyone does.

> Give me freedom from television because I'm beginning to distrust its happy endings.
>
> Give me sex education to correct what I first heard from thirteen year olds.
>
> Give me homework to keep from flunking Free Time.
>
> Give me a map of the world so I may see that this town and I aren't the center of it.
>
> Give me the knowledge that conformity is the enemy of friendship.
>
> Give me the understanding that nobody ever grows up in a group, so I may find my own way.
>
> Give me limits so I will know I'm loved.
>
> And give me nothing I haven't earned so that this adolescence doesn't last forever.
>
> Amen. 3

Peck sometimes finds himself frustrated by the values of today's teenagers, but he also cares about them and wants to give them some kind of hope and direction. Despite the many distractions and sources of entertainment available to teens, he believes a good book is still important and is a way to connect with a person in a meaningful, personal way. Peck's books encourage independence and responsibility. Peck explains: "I'd failed as a teacher. I'd never convinced enough students that they didn't know what they thought until they'd written it down, that books provide alternatives, that fiction can be truer than fact. But teaching made a writer out of me. It gave me a priceless viewpoint for a writer: to pay more attention to what people do than to what they say."[4]

In many ways, Peck is still a teacher. "I think I'm still teaching English," he admits. "I'm looking for stories where I used to look for lesson plans, somewhere in the lives of my readers."[5] His books entertain, all the while providing young people with knowledge, direction, and hope.

How does he know what to write about; how does he know what will interest today's youth? Peck is not the kind of writer who is always alone at his desk. He makes an effort to go out into the schools and spend time with the students. He feels it is important to stay in touch with the generation for which he is writing. Peck spends about a quarter of the year traveling to schools around the country and getting to know the students.

Although Peck's books cover a wide range of subjects, he almost always writes about kids who do not conform to their peer groups, kids who are independent and responsible. He explains, "Not every novel is told against the backdrop of the peer group, though we need every one that is. We need no novels about how to fit in. Popularity and acceptance cost too much now."[6] Through his strong characters, Peck tries to instill a sense of independence and responsibility.

Peck has been a full-time writer for 30 years, resulting in the publication of more than 30 novels for children, young adults, and adults. He has made a strong and lasting impact on young adult literature.

A 1949 photo of boys selling sodas to save bears in Decatur, Illinois, Richard Peck's hometown. Peck has described his boyhood during the 1940s as somewhat idyllic and a far cry from the pressures children face in the modern world.

2

A Quiet Childhood

RICHARD PECK WAS born on April 5, 1934, in Decatur, a town in Illinois located about 180 miles south of Chicago.

He grew up in a very different time, in a place that was like something out of a Norman Rockwell painting. He lived in a white frame house on Dennis Avenue next to Fairview Park with his mother and father. He was an only child until he reached the third grade, when his sister, Cheryl, was born. In his neighborhood, the brick streets were tree lined, and many of the homes were Victorian and Dutch colonial houses with enormous porches. There was also an 1829 courthouse with a plaque honoring Abraham Lincoln. Decatur was Lincoln's first home in Illinois; he and his family had moved there in 1831. When Peck was living in Decatur, it was a small town with a strong sense of community. The various generations and classes all lived together. Though there were rich kids and poor kids, and they were certainly aware of this, especially later in high school, it did not seem to have a great effect on them. Everyone went to the same school, where the teachers treated them equally.

Peck's mother, Virginia Gray, was a trained dietician and made an art of home-cooked meals. She was a graduate of Illinois Wesleyan University. Peck's father, Wayne M. Peck, often hunted and fished, bringing home pheasants and catfish for Virginia to cook. She would test recipes and then compile them in volumes. His father had been raised on a farm. He dropped out of school before he reached the seventh grade. He then hopped freight trains to the Dakotas, where he joined in the wheat harvest. He fought in World War I and returned partially disabled with a shattered left shoulder. Now unable to farm, he ran a Phillips 66 gas station. Instead of putting on a suit in the morning to go to work, Peck's father would drive off on his Harley-Davidson motorcycle.

Peck was part of a large extended family, with many of his relatives living close by. His maternal great-grandfather, William Gray, an Irish immigrant, had bought a farm in western Illinois in 1852, which he passed down to his son, John, who farmed it until 1964. It was called the Walnut Grove Farm. Peck enjoyed visiting the farm as a kid. He would listen to his grandparents and great-aunts tell stories of the past; these stories left a strong impression on him. Peck was born in the midst of the Great Depression (which began in 1929), or, as he recalled it, "I'd been born after the party was over."[1] His grandmother, Flossie Mae Gray, and her four sisters, Pearl, Mura, Maude, and Ozena, liked to spin entertaining yarns, recalling the good times. Peck was an observant child and a good listener. He still has many memories of his aunts' stories, which later influenced his writing. "Writing is the art of listening," he explains. "On many subjects women are more verbal than men. More accessible. I can clearly remember my great aunts' voices. I can remember the tone, the timbre of their voices, and some of their phrases. I can't remember my uncles who sat quietly and listened."[2]

An exception to this was his great-uncle on his father's side of the family, Miles Peck, who told colorful stories. Peck describes his eccentric great-uncle as a carpenter in his eighties who "terrorized the town in his Model A Ford fitted with a carpentry box where the rumble seat had been." Miles "was in business for himself and considered other people's privacy fair game." Peck, as a young child, "thought he was God."[3]

Peck heard many entertaining stories from the men who stopped by his father's gas station, as well. He would eavesdrop on the conversations of these truckers, farmers, and railroaders. He also overheard the talk of the 12-year-old newspaper delivery boys who came into the gas station to roll their papers. Peck listened to stories his father told, about his years as a kid. "He stayed a country boy in his heart, and his stories mingled with Mark Twain's in my mind," Peck said. "That was one of my first links between reality, or at least memory, and what happens in books. I saw Huckleberry Finn as a father figure."[4] One of his all-time favorite authors, as a child and as an adult, is Mark Twain.

It was not until years later that Peck realized just how useful all of these stories would be for his writing. It is important that a writer is observant. Many writers start paying attention at a young age, without even realizing that they are training themselves. Peck explains, "I was gathering material long before I knew what to do with it. Writers and children are natural snoops, though writers call it 'research.' Had I known how brief childhood is, I'd have looked closer."[5]

LIFE DURING WARTIME

Peck grew up during World War II, a time of war shortages and rationing. He entered kindergarten on the day the German army invaded Poland in 1939. He used to listen to the adults discuss the war and find the foreign places they were talking about on maps. This curiosity taught him early on that Decatur was not the center of the universe, but only a small dot on the map. Although Peck liked the town in which he was raised, he also knew there were many other places he wanted to see. When Peck was in the fifth grade, Europe celebrated V-E Day, victory in Europe, on May 8, 1945. A few months later, in August, the war in the Pacific ended when the United States dropped atomic bombs on Japan.

Peck wanted to see the world—he especially wanted to see New York City, which he knew must be a much different place from quaint Decatur. In fact, Peck started to dream about New York at a very young age. When he was in preschool, each day the piano teacher, Miss Beth Butts, would ask a different child to choose a song and she would play it on the piano. Any song that the child picked, she would play in march time. When it was Peck's turn, he chose "Sidewalks of New York." Surprised, she asked him why he picked that particular song. He responded:

> "Because I'll be moving to New York."
>
> "Really?" She knew my parents well and how firmly rooted they were. "Soon?"
>
> "Well, as soon as I can get there," I said.[6]

Peck was a child during the golden age of radio. He would lie in front of a Philco radio and listen to broadcasts, dreaming of being a writer and being in London or New York. Many years later, as an adult, Peck would achieve that dream.

Did you know...

The Ghost Belonged to Me was turned into a Walt Disney movie called *Child of Glass* that aired on television for the "Wonderful World of Disney" in 1978. Peck had no say in the script, but he did get to tour the Disney studios. Other television movies based on Peck's books include *Are You in the House Alone?* (CBS, 1977) and *Father Figure* (1980). *Father Figure* was produced by David Susskin, and Jim was played by the young Timothy Hutton. *Don't Look and It Won't Hurt* (1972) was made into a movie called *Gas Food Lodging* in 1992. In the movie version, the older sister refuses to come back home. She plans to go to Dallas to become a model.

AN EARLY LOVE OF READING

Reading also sparked Peck's imagination about the world. Peck's mother often read to him. She also taught him the alphabet at a young age so that he could write thank-you letters to his grandparents and relatives after receiving birthday and Christmas gifts. Peck states, "Because she intoxicated me with words, I entered grade school with a vocabulary I can't find in the letters ninth graders send to me now."[7] Some of Peck's favorite books when he was young were the fairy tales of the Brothers Grimm—German brothers who wrote many now-famous fairy tales in the early 1800s, including "Cinderella." He also loved the adventure stories of Richard Halliburton, an "American gentleman adventurer" who resembled an old-fashioned Indiana Jones.[8] Peck looked forward to the monthly arrival of *National Geographic* as well. When he looked at the pictures of the foreign places in the magazine, he felt himself transported.

Although Peck believes that writing can be taught, he also believes it involves a love of reading and words, which usually starts in childhood. Peck has repeatedly stressed: "Nobody but a reader ever became a writer."[9] Peck has always loved reading. Reading helped develop Peck's imagination and encouraged him to dream about other worlds, which led him on the path to becoming a writer. Peck says about himself and fellow writers, "I suspect we all began early in childhood."[10]

Peck attended Woodrow Wilson Junior High School. He always completed his homework, attended classes, and made good grades. Still, reading and schoolwork did not take up all of his time. Peck was wild about cars and, at a very young age, felt proud that he could instantly identify the make and model of each car coming into his father's gas station. In the mornings, Peck delivered papers and from this job learned the importance of responsibility. He also attended Miss Van Dykes's Fortnightly Dancing Class, where he learned to waltz, foxtrot, and rhumba. He was a tall kid, already six feet in the seventh grade. Despite his size, Peck was not much of an athlete, but he was good at dancing. In the eighth grade, he attended high school dances wearing a double-breasted Palm Beach white dinner jacket.

After junior high, Peck went to Stephen Decatur High School, where he continued to study hard and make good grades. Later, he cited important subjects like history, Latin, and geography in helping him develop as a writer. By this time, Peck was already thinking about becoming a writer, but he did not tell anyone. He did not know how to go about it—there were no writers living in Decatur to learn from. How could a boy from Decatur be a writer? How could he see the world?

NEW EXPERIENCES

Two significant events in Peck's high school years caused him to begin thinking more seriously about writing. First, during junior year, his English teacher announced that the sister of Vachel Lindsay, a poet from Illinois, would be reading his poetry at a nearby college. Lindsay was no longer alive, but he had grown up in Springfield, the next town over, and it was an eye-opener for Peck to realize that there were writers who came from central Illinois. This meant it could be done. Peck attended the reading. When Lindsay's sister, Olive Lindsay Wakefield, who was in her eighties, read her late brother's poetry, she also performed, beginning to jig and then to dance. It was quite memorable. A few weeks later, Peck stopped by and visited with her. She was his only living link to a real writer.

Second, Peck experienced life outside of Decatur, Illinois, when he spent a summer in New York City. A distant relative living in the city invited Peck to visit during the summer. Peck, who was then sixteen, had wanted to go to New York since he was in preschool. He took on odd jobs around the neighborhood, raking leaves and doing yard work, until he had saved enough money for a train ticket. That summer, Peck soaked in as much as he could—the magnitude of the city, the tall buildings, and the diversity of people. New York City stunned him with its grandness, but at the same time, he felt right at home. He explored the different neighborhoods and rode the subway all the way to Coney Island.

During his senior year, Peck was inducted into the National Honor Society. Then, in 1952, he won a Rector Scholarship, which aided in his acceptance to DePauw University in Greencastle, Indiana. Peck was able to avoid the draft because he was enrolled in college. At that time, once a man turned 18, unless he attended college and remained in the upper half of his class, he was likely to be drafted and sent to fight in the Korean War. This was a civil war between North and South Korea; the United States supported South Korea against the communist North. The war, which began on June 25, 1950, ended in 1953.

Peck still wanted to be a writer, but he knew that this was a difficult profession to pursue: "Even though I'd thought there was a novelist in me, I'd come from Illinois where we were raised to make livings, not take chances."[11] Instead, he decided to major in education. He planned to be an English teacher, which he thought could bring him closer to literature. He also wanted to help young people expand their worlds. He thought that teaching was one of the country's most important and necessary

A photo of the East College building, one of the oldest on DePauw University's campus. While attending the university, Peck decided to become a teacher instead of a writer, because he believed that he needed to be practical about his future career.

professions and felt inspired by the many good teachers he had encountered in his life.

One of those teachers was Miss F., Peck's senior year composition teacher. He recalled an informative experience with Miss F: He was accustomed to receiving As on his compositions. When Miss F. returned his first paper, there was no grade on it. Instead, she had written across the page, "Never express yourself again on my time. Find a more interesting topic." Peck, then just 17, did not know what she meant. He went to her and asked, "What would a more interesting topic be?" She replied, "Almost anything."[12] These words stayed with Peck for all of his life. He went to the library and began to research. He learned that he did not have to write about himself. There were many other topics and subjects—this insight opened his world.

The summer before his junior year of college, Peck worked as a dishwasher at George Williams College Camp on Lake Geneva, in Wisconsin, saving money for the trip he would soon take. Peck had been dreaming of faraway places for a long time, and he finally had the opportunity to live in a place on the other side of the Atlantic Ocean. Peck spent his junior year at the University of Exeter in England. In the fall of 1954, he sailed across the Atlantic aboard the *Ile de France*. The journey and the year in England left a strong impression on Peck.

Exeter University is set in a medieval town in the southwest of England, surrounded by rolling farmland and old, impressive buildings. It was a very different place from Decatur. Peck studied literature and British history and became close friends with the other boys. There were only about 10 American students at the school. Peck was beginning to get a better sense of just how large and diverse the world is, and he knew that traveling was something he wanted to experience throughout his lifetime.

He returned home to finish his senior year and received his B.A. degree from DePauw University in 1956. Next, Peck found himself in the U.S. Army, where he spent two years. Even though his draft had been deferred, he still had to enlist after he graduated from college. Peck completed basic training at Fort Carson, Colorado, and then was stationed just outside Ansbach, in what was then

West Germany. He worked as the company clerk/typist and, because of his good writing skills, often ghostwrote sermons for the chaplains. The chaplains were impressed by his sermons, and soon Peck was recruited as a chaplain's assistant and posted to Stuttgart. Peck continued to write sermons and also acted as a marriage counselor. He heard many confessions and realized later that this was where he "learned that writing was going to be the art of listening."[13] While in the army and in graduate school, Peck explored Europe. He visited Rome, Italy; Bruges, Belgium; and London, England, hitchhiking and meeting interesting people, as well as learning how to be alone—a key element for a writer.

Peck attended graduate school at Southern Illinois University at Carbondale, and completed his work at Washington University. While he was in graduate school, he served as a teaching assistant, teaching writing to freshmen. The first time he taught, he expected to walk into a classroom of 18-year-olds, but instead the class was made up of older adults who were taking an evening class. He was the youngest person in the room. He said, "I fell for teaching on the first night."[14] Peck earned his master's degree in 1959.

After he received his degree, he continued to teach at Southern Illinois University as an instructor in English. Then, in the fall of 1961, he began to teach English in a public high school. Teaching, Peck soon found out, was not exactly what he had been expecting. For his first high school teaching job, Peck taught at Glenbrook North High School in the affluent Chicago suburb of Northbrook, Illinois—it was an experience that would leave him a changed man.

A photo of Hunter College High School on the Upper East Side of New York City, where Peck taught until he decided to embark on a writing career.

3

In the Classroom

PECK ARRIVED IN the classroom full of energy and high expectations. He was surprised and disappointed by what he encountered. Glenbrook North High School did not at all resemble his own experience of school in Decatur. The students at Glenbrook seemed undisciplined, unchallenged, and self-centered. Peck observed how much influence their peer groups wielded over them. He felt discouraged by the emphasis on class and money. Later, this wealthy high school would provide the setting for his tenth young adult novel, *Close Enough to Touch.*

After two years of teaching, Peck decided he needed a change. He found a job as a textbook editor for Scott, Foresman and Company in Chicago. While there, he also did a little writing of his own. He and a friend wrote a guide to Chicago nightlife called *Old Town, A Complete Guide: Strolling, Shopping, Supping, Sipping*, which they self-published in 1965. Though the book was fairly trivial, it still tapped into Peck's desire to write. It was his first published work.

TEACHING IN NEW YORK

After two years in Chicago, Peck fulfilled his long-time dream of living in New York City. When he was 32, he was hired to teach English and education courses at Hunter College and its laboratory school, Hunter College High School, an all-girls high school for the gifted, located on the Upper East Side of Manhattan.

Peck had high hopes that teaching in New York would be different from what he had experienced at Glenbrook. In some ways it was different, but much of it was the same, such as the permissive school administrators and the heavy influence of peers. Also, because he was teaching "gifted" students, Peck felt that the students did not want to learn anything. They acted as if they already knew everything there was to know. Peck observed that the students needed more direction, and the schools were letting them down: "But we'd long since begun raising grades and lowering expectations to make winners out of everybody."[1]

Peck was teaching in the late 1960s, a socially and politically turbulent time in America. In addition to dealing with racial unrest, the country was also deeply involved in the Vietnam War, which lasted until the early 1970s. American soldiers were sent to Vietnam, in Southeast

A crowd of young people wade into the reflecting pool on the Mall facing the Washington Monument in Washington, D.C., as part of a protest demonstration against the Vietnam War, on May 9, 1970. As a teacher during this period, Peck often found it difficult to teach students who preferred to go to protests than attend classes and who experimented freely with drugs.

Asia, to fight against the spread of communism. The war lasted more than 10 years and was very unpopular with the American public. There were many protests about the war across the United States, particularly in New York. If students went to the protests instead of class, Hunter did not reprimand them. In Peck's view, this made effective teaching difficult to do. Also during this time period, young people freely experimented with drugs. Peck recalled a scary time when one of his students dropped out of her seat into the aisle and had to be rushed to the hospital because of a drug overdose.

In general, Peck felt as if the school administration had given up. The atmosphere was too permissive, and the students were not getting the guidance they needed. "Somewhere in the 1960s the tide turned, and power shifted from adults to children," attests Peck.[2] Peck is known for his strong, expressive views on the failure of the American education system. When he was in school, he recalls, there was a sense of authority. He feels that too much of teaching today focuses on nurturing the students' self-esteem. While this may be important, Peck believes it is even more crucial to focus on actually *teaching*, on expanding and sharpening minds.

Peck also recognizes that it was easier to be a teacher when he was a kid, as it was also easier to be a kid. The problems that often plague schools today, such as drugs and guns, did not yet exist. At that time, teachers were also a part of the community—they lived in the town in which they taught.

After adjusting to high school students, Peck was assigned to teach junior high. He jokes, "Nobody chooses to teach junior high. You get assigned."[3] Now Peck had to start again from scratch, coming up with a new curriculum and trying to find appropriate books for his students to read. Back then, there were not many books geared toward young teens. Peck came up with a list of what he hoped would be appropriate reading material. He recalled that, on the day he began to teach junior high, the English faculty decided to ban Harper Lee's *To Kill a*

Mockingbird, one of the books on his list for the students to read, because it celebrated "white bourgeois values." Peck, adamantly against censorship and book banning, realized this might actually have the opposite of its intended

Did you know...

Although Richard Peck does not like technology and types his work on an old-fashioned typewriter, he has written two popular books featuring technology—*Lost in Cyberspace* and its sequel, *The Great Interactive Dream Machine*. The books are told from the eyes of two New York City, Upper East Side private-school boys. The boys time-travel to the past, but there is a glitch, and every time they return, they bring someone from the past back with them. Peck says:

"Like a lot of adults, I noticed that 12 year olds are already far more computer-literate than I will ever be. As a writer, I could create a funny story on the subject, but I expect young readers will be more attracted to it because it is also a story about two friends having adventures together. There's a touch of time travel in it, too, cybernetically speaking, for those readers who liked sharing Blossom Culp's exploits."*

* "Richard Peck." Penguin.com (USA). Available online. URL: http://us.penguingroup.com/nf/Author/AuthorPage/0,,1000025091,00.html.

effect. He explained, "I did the only thing I could think of. I entered my classroom, wrote title and author across the blackboard, and told the eighth-graders the simple truth—that the book on the board had been removed for their well-being."[4]

That was one book the students read.

Peck ran into many walls teaching junior high, but he also enjoyed the students and wanted to make a difference in their lives. He found that, most of the time, he was "hung up between laughter and tears."[5] Peck was a good teacher—committed, knowledgeable, and funny. There were many days that left him disappointed, however. After one of these days, Peck went home from school and wrote a poem called "Nancy," a period piece of those times and a sketch of that generation, which was published in the *Saturday Review.*

CHANGING PROFESSIONS

Peck received tenure at Hunter but felt like he wanted to do something else, something that would have more of an effect on the world of education. Then he won a one-year Harold L. Clapp Fellowship, which gave him the title of assistant director of the Council for Basic Education in Washington, D.C. The Council for Basic Education is a small, privately funded organization that monitors and evaluates educational innovations. In 1969, the group focused on English education. Peck wrote a monthly newsletter for the organization; he also went into the schools and sat in classrooms, observing different teaching methods and programs.

The break from teaching was what Peck needed. He now knew he wanted to leave the profession and try writing full time. Peck had continued to write and edit to some extent over the course of his teaching career. Early on, when he started teaching at Hunter, one of his colleagues, Ned Hoopes, invited Peck to help him with a manuscript. Together, they put together a book called *Edge of Awareness: Twenty-Five Contemporary Essays.* Peck received $730 for it, but, more importantly, this book brought him into the world of publishing in New York. He met George Nicholson, a young editor who would become one of the leading figures in the business of publishing books for children and young adults. Nicholson would later publish Peck's first novel.

During this time, Peck wrote a column on the architecture of historic neighborhoods for the *New York Times* and contributed articles to the *Chicago Tribune* and the *Saturday Review of Literature.* In 1970, Peck published a poetry anthology that he edited called *Sounds and Silences: Poetry for Now.* A second poetry anthology, *Mindscapes*, was published in 1971. Both books consisted of poems by contemporary poets, including a few of Peck's own poems. Even after he wrote his first novel, Peck continued to write occasional articles on travel, history, and architecture, publishing in the *Saturday Review*, *House Beautiful*, *American Libraries*, and the *New York Times.* Writing young adult novels, however, was what he *wanted* to do.

When Peck returned to Hunter, he knew that he wanted to try to be a writer full time. He felt like there was nothing else he could offer his students. At this time, there were still very few books geared toward teenagers. Peck wanted to write books that his students would like. It would not be until many years later that young adult literature would become such a popular market.

WRITING THAT FIRST BOOK

On his return to the classroom, Peck observed that nothing had changed—in fact, things may have become even worse. His desire to write was growing, as were his frustrations with teaching. Peck did the only thing he felt he could do: after he taught one more semester, he turned in his resignation. He recalls, "I left teaching, but not lightly, because I knew I wasn't coming back."[6] He went home after his last day in the classroom, and he began to write his first novel. He explained: "I wrote it one word at a time, feeling my way down many a dead end, just as I've written all the rest: pausing for an agonizing reappraisal at the foot of every page, spotting for the unnecessary word, the prewilted image, writing six drafts. Marveling at how much harder it is to write a novel than to teach one, how much easier to criticize than create."[7]

Don't Look and It Won't Hurt was published by Holt, Rinehart & Winston. The novel was a critical success and is still popular with readers today.

Peck took a big risk by quitting his job to become a writer. Many writers have other jobs with which they support themselves and cannot quit until they have had many books published. For example, the late young adult author Paula Danziger, who wrote *The Cat Ate My Gymsuit*, among many other popular books, was a classroom teacher until her novels sold well enough to allow her to quit and write full time. The late Robert Cormier was a newspaper writer and editor when his first novels were published. Ann Martin, the author of the Baby-sitters Club books, worked as an editor and did not leave her job until she had already published five books.

Richard Peck gave up his teaching career before he even wrote the first line. He had no expectations, but he knew he had to try.

Above, Richard Peck holds a magazine he signed for a fan. Peck's connection with his fans, aided by his frequent visits to schools and libraries, is part of the reason why his books remain relevant to his readers.

4

What Teens Teach Him

PECK BEGAN TO miss teaching soon after he left. He could not stop thinking about the students. The very source of his frustration was also the source of his artistic inspiration. Peck knew who he wanted to write about and who he was writing for. According to his biographer, Richard Gallo:

> Although Richard Peck felt he had not taught his students very much, he knew his students had provided him with almost all of the material he needed to get started as a young adult novelist. First, he had an insider's view of how teenagers behaved, dressed, talked, and interacted as well as what they valued. Second, he had

> learned what young people like and want in a book: they want to be entertained, and they want to be reassured.[1]

When Peck wrote his first few novels, he recalled his students—what they said, what they wore, what they looked like. Eventually, however, his memories began to fade. How could he capture the lives of students without being in touch with them? Peck felt it was important to know what students were talking about—their dreams, fears, and concerns. He wanted to know what made them tick. So Peck started going into the schools. He joined author-in-the-school programs and gave talks and readings, all the while observing students in classrooms, libraries, and hallways.

VISITING SCHOOLS, GETTING INSPIRATION

Traveling to schools has become a regular part of Peck's life. Today, he speaks in up to 60 schools and libraries each year, talking with teachers, librarians, and students. He travels for almost a quarter of every year. He goes to schools and communities, talking to students to find out their concerns, worries, likes, and dislikes. This proves to be an invaluable part of his writing process.

Peck travels approximately 60,000 miles each year for his work. He has visited affluent suburban schools, poor inner-city high schools, and middle-class rural schools, in places as diverse as Connecticut, Ohio, Colorado, and Alaska. Wherever he goes, he makes sure he spends time talking with the students, observing them, and listening to them.

Setting and teenage culture are very important in Peck's books. He often dresses his characters in contemporary fashion, with references to name brands. For example, in his 1980s novels, such as *Close Enough to Touch*, characters wear Jordache jeans and Nike and Puma sneakers. In *Strays Like Us*, published in 1998, Peck describes the kids who show up to school: "You saw everything—black lipstick, nose rings, baremiddles. And a lot of people too jumpy to sit down . . . a lot of low-crotch denim and novelty haircuts and words written on their hands."[2] Peck also feels it is important to listen to how teenagers talk, in order to capture their vocabulary and slang. He is very careful about finding their voices.

For his novel *Princess Ashley*, which deals with themes of conformity and parent-child relationships, he based the storyline on a wealthy high school where he had been a visiting author. At the school, Peck would walk down the hall to eavesdrop and take notes. He explained, "I wanted nothing in the novel that wasn't directly based on what was in fact happening among the students in that school, their patterns and parties, their home lives and school lives, the vast open stretches of their free time."[3] Peck also relied on information from a teenage daughter of his friends, who provided him with helpful details about many of the students.

Peck is often invited to give talks at schools. He is a good speaker and enjoys the group interaction. When Peck was in high school, public speaking made him nervous. In college, when he was at Exeter, a professor assigned him to give a 10-minute presentation at a local grammar school. Peck was nervous, but he gave the presentation, and afterward he realized, "I was cured. Being on stage was less agonizing than hiding."[4] Peck got over his fear of speaking and now enjoys it. Writing is such an act of solitude that it can bc quite lonely. Speaking to groups gives Peck a break from that solitude. "Teaching had made this new career possible, but it hadn't taught me how to sit alone in an empty room without bells," he admitted. "I missed the shape of the school day. I missed colleagues and young voices."[5]

On his school visits, Peck gives helpful advice to students and expounds on his strong viewpoints. He is quick with responses and has many sharp one-liners, such as, "Watching television is what you do with your life when you don't want to live it."[6] Peck is full of advice for young writers. He recommends that students study Latin and learn five new words every day. He also suggests that, if you want to be a writer, you read 1,000 books before you start writing. "No one became a writer before they became a reader," he says.[7]

When Peck started visiting schools, he remembered from his teaching days how valuable the students' compositions could be. In their papers, the students were often more honest about what they were feeling. Now, before he visits classrooms, he asks the teacher to assign compositions and then mail them to him in advance. For a topic, he often asks the students to write about, "something that happened to me that would fit into a novel." With this assignment, Peck gets students writing about their problems. Sometimes, they might write about the death of a grandparent or the death of an older sister or brother in a drunk driving accident.

Did you know...

Peck's adult novel *Amanda/Miranda* was translated into nine languages and printed in special editions by the Literary Guild and *Reader's Digest*, as well as in Braille. It took him four years to write *Amanda/Miranda*. Peck then rewrote it 20 years later in a more streamlined version for young readers. Peck's other novels for adults include *New York Time*, *London Holiday*, and *This Family of Women*.

Peck puts a significant amount of time and preparatory work into his school visits and always provides helpful, encouraging comments on the papers the students write for him. The compositions help Peck get to know the students and may give him ideas for what to write about next. He has observed over the years that it is not just what the students say in their compositions but also what they do not say: "Their silences are as telling as their words, and I'm moved to write what they won't," he explains.[8] Sometimes, he finds inspiration for a novel in the students' compositions. For example, one particular composition that popped out at him was written by a girl whose father had left her family. Peck thought about this girl for a long time, and then he decided to write about her. This turned into the novel *Unfinished Portrait of Jessica.*

When Peck is traveling to schools across the country, he is essentially conducting research, finding inspiration, and getting ideas for his fiction. He states: "I get ideas for my stories in schools where I go to visit. Some kid, somewhere, always tells me what my next book is going to be about. And some teacher tells me about something that is going on with young people in that community that nobody else knows and that no parent would dare to know."[9]

Peck hears stories from the teachers and the students themselves. His best ideas for books come directly from the students and what he notices about them on his travels. For instance, early on in his career, he went to a school in a western city where all but a couple of the boys in the class lived without fathers. He thought about what this would be like, for a boy to grow up without his father. Peck did not know how this would feel, because he had grown up with his father. As a writer, though, he puts himself in other people's shoes and thinks about situations from their points of view. Later, he realized that he could relate, on a certain level. He explains: "Nothing in my coming-of-age or family prepared me to write their story. Or did it? Confronting a generation of boys without fathers when I couldn't fathom growing up without my own may have been the novel's real inspiration. On the day I finished it my father died, and at forty-three I was as lost as I would have been at any moment before."[10]

The book was *Father Figure,* about Jim, a 17-year-old boy struggling to grow up after his father leaves the family. Jim tries to make up for this loss by playing the father-figure role for his little brother, Byron. The brothers live in Brooklyn, New York, but, after their mother dies, they are sent away to Florida to live with their father, a man they hardly know.

WHERE HE GETS HIS IDEAS

Peck also gets ideas from reading other books. For example, he likes to read biographies, which sometimes give him ideas for characters. Fiction has also been an inspiration. He describes his Blossom Culp character as being partly inspired by Mark Twain's Huckleberry Finn. In addition to what Peck saw at the school where the boys were growing up without fathers, Judith Guest's *Ordinary People* (1976) also inspired him to write *Father Figure. Ordinary People* is about a son's death and how the family, especially the younger brother, deal with their grief. When Peck read the book, he started thinking about the relationships between brothers, sons, and fathers.

Sometimes, Peck's own books have led him to the next one. For example, *Father Figure* led to *Close Enough to Touch*, because he wanted to "give boys an emotional voice."[11] He also wrote *Close Enough to Touch* because once a young man asked him to write a book about dating, and *Close Enough to Touch* is a love story that is told from the boy's perspective. With this book, Peck wanted to write about a male character who was able to communicate his emotions. Interestingly, his readers' reactions to *Close Enough to Touch* led to his next book.

After he wrote *Close Enough to Touch*, Peck went around the country to discuss the book with students. He would go to the classroom and read the first two scenes of the book, which portray Matt's declaration of love to Dory. He then would reveal to the students that Dory later dies and ask them what a boy in Matt's situation might do. Peck was shocked by the response: In every class, someone said that Matt could end his grief by killing himself. This startling reaction led Peck to write *Remembering the Good Times*, which confronts the issue of teenage suicide.

By 1985, suicide was one of the three major killers of young people. Peck researched the subject extensively and visited schools in Plano, Texas; Westchester County, New York; and Beverly Hills, California. He also went to suicide-prevention programs and talked with suicide hotline volunteers. He initially tried to write the novel from the point of view of Trav, the boy who kills himself, but this did not work. Peck decided that if Trav could express himself, then maybe he would not reach the desperate point of suicide. He realized the story was better told from the point of view of a friend. Peck also knew that he could not just list the symptoms of a suicide-prone teen—"a novel has to be something more than a warning."[12] He chose to also make it a story about friendship. This novel—which received more reviews than any of Peck's previous books—also deals with other realistic subjects that come up in many of his works: the loneliness of the suburbs, conformity, class differences, inadequacies of schools, and the need for caring adults in teenagers' lives.

Letters to Peck from his readers have also been important sources of inspiration. Often students write letters to him for a school assignment, but occasionally he receives a letter from a young person who just feels like writing to him—these are the best kind. Peck explains how letters can be important sources of inspiration: "I'm also under the influence of letters because sometimes it's the lonely who write. They want to talk to somebody and you're it. They usually want to talk to you because something has happened in the book that makes them think that you are near enough to hear them but far enough away to be safe. That's important."[13]

DISCOVERING MALLS

In the mid-1970s, Peck was getting letters from his readers in which they often mentioned hanging out at the mall. He did not know what they were talking about. At the time, Peck knew nothing about malls—there were no shopping malls where he lived in New York City, and they were just beginning to become popular across the United States. So one day he took his notebook, headed to the Port Authority in Manhattan, and took a bus to New Jersey. He soon found himself standing in the gigantic parking lot of Paramus Park. "A vision of hell," he recalled. "I went that day to the mall, where nothing but letters could have sent me, to shop for a novel."[14]

Peck realized that the mall was the center of activity in the suburbs. On his travels, he began dropping into malls across the country. He explains that he could find his audience at the mall, which "became metaphor of coming of age, suburban, consumerist, and climate-controlled, the place to buy your disguises where no adult is truly in charge."[15]

The escalators in the Brent Cross Shopping Centre in England, in 1976. Because he had grown up in a small town and lived his adult life in New York City, Peck had little understanding of malls. When they became popular hangouts for young people in the 1970s, both in the United States and Great Britain, Peck began to write about them.

Peck wrote seven drafts of a novel about the mall, then reread it once more and realized he had gotten it wrong. He had written it more for himself than for his students. In this version, all of the characters died in the parking lot. "I'd broken a rule. I'd left my readers without hope, and you can't do that."[16] He also admits, "Nobody likes too much bad news in a novel, and this was nothing but."[17] Peck fed the novel to the fireplace and turned to writing something else. Over the next two years, however, references to malls continued to pop up, so he decided to rewrite the novel. He changed the tone and this time wrote a satire called *Secrets of the Shopping Mall.* He brought in two characters from the past—Priscilla and Melvin, the largest girl and the smallest boy in the school, from his short story "Priscilla and the Wimps." He renamed them Teresa and Barnie. With only four dollars between them, they hop a bus and ride to the end of the line, Paradise Park, which turns out to be a cement-covered suburban shopping mall. With no money and no home to return to, they are forced to stay. Barnie and Teresa spend their days and nights in a large department store. Just when they think they can live there unnoticed forever, they find out they are not alone.

The book was different from Peck's more serious works. Critics did not respond as well as they had to previous books, but the novel was very popular with his readers. It was translated into several languages and continues to be one of his best-selling books.

TACKLING TOUGH TOPICS

Peck also bases his books on serious issues that are in the news. For example, he wrote about rape in the 1970s, when it was one of the fastest-growing, least-reported crimes. He reviewed several nonfiction books about rape and started imagining a girl living in the suburbs, who had no street smarts and who would never believe that someone from her peer group would hurt her. Peck wrote *Are You in the House Alone?,* in which a high school girl is stalked and raped by a classmate. It was such a shift from his early novels that Peck was afraid it could ruin his career, but critics praised the book, and it continues to be an important book for many readers.

In it, Gail, a junior in high school, is harassed by anonymous phone calls and letters. One night while she is babysitting, she opens the door. A boy from high school is standing there—and what happens next will forever change her. Peck does not write the rape scene, but he does write about the medical examination that follows in graphic detail. Peck felt it was important to write this scene because many rape victims do not go in for a medical examination. Many people in the community want Gail to put it all behind her, or they blame her instead of the rapist, who comes from a well-respected family.

Peck wanted to portray the harsh reality of rape—that, unfortunately, there is not always justice, and the rapist is not always held accountable. "I wrote *Are You in the House Alone*? to indicate that life is not a television show," he explains.[18] Peck found it ironic that the book was actually made into a TV movie starring a young Dennis Quaid as the rapist. Peck had no control over the script. He first knew the film was finished when he saw the listing in *TV Guide*. Peck was disappointed by the easy ending. Just before the final commercial, the rapist is caught and separated from society: On TV, unlike real life, there is easy justice.

Richard Peck's protagonists are often the least-popular kids in school—the loners who are apart from the popular crowds, but who are also not afraid to take action when necessary. Because of their perspectives as outsiders, these characters often have a lot to say about the world we live in.

5

The Young and the Old

FROM HIS MANY years of observing students, Peck has concluded that a great many young people worry about winning the approval of their peers and that they have trouble standing up for themselves. Contrarily, in his books, Peck writes about characters who do not follow the group mentality.

Usually, Peck's protagonists, the main characters of the book, do not come from upper-class homes. They are not the most talented in the group or the most popular in school. They are often on the outside already, but they are also strong characters who are not afraid to take action. Peck explains that "from my first novel about an imperfect family I learned that the protagonist of a young-adult novel is not the case study or the victim. The protagonist is the young person who acts."[1]

Peck hopes that his readers can relate to his characters. He believes characters should resemble real people. However, a character in a book might also be more likely to stand up for him- or herself, or may be able to express ideas or emotions better than most young people do in real life. Peck elaborates, with sly humor: "The main characters of books for the young have new jobs to perform. They're even linguistic role models. They can speak the length of a book without ever saying 'like' or 'you know.' Our characters speak as our readers would if they had the immediate and radical speech correction they need."[2]

Peck does not write his novels for the popular jock or the leaders of the student council. He writes his books for the loners, the students on the edge of the crowd, and the unpopular kids. Peck portrays characters that the young can look up to. He has also come to the conclusion that most young people do not want to read about characters their own age, but about young people who are a couple of years older.

BRINGING BLOSSOM CULP TO LIFE

When Peck wrote *The Ghost Belonged to Me*, which takes place in the first decade of the twentieth century, he made Alexander Armsworth the protagonist of the story and Blossom Culp a secondary character. Blossom is unpopular, unattractive, poor, and from the wrong side of the tracks. Her alcoholic father has left town, and her mother is a witch. Blossom is also unique. She can travel through time and has the gift of second sight—the ability to see the future. Blossom is also adventuresome and resourceful, and in her, Peck says, she has "more than a hint of Huckleberry Finn."[3]

Blossom is an independent character, the kind of character Peck thinks is important for his readers to see. "Blossom will never be a joiner as long as I live," Peck attests.[4]

Blossom Culp was one of his favorite characters to develop, and quickly became his most popular character. After the novel was published, Peck received more fan letters about Blossom than about Alexander, the main character. Kids liked and responded to Blossom's plucky and adventurous attitude. In response, after the first book, Peck decided that Alexander would become the sidekick, and Blossom became the main character. The next three novels about Blossom are *Ghosts I Have Been*; *The Dreadful Future of Blossom Culp*; and *Blossom Culp and the Sleep of Death*. Both the first and second books in the series won much praise from critics. The third book, *The Dreadful Future of Blossom Culp*, did not win reviewers over in the same way, however. Interestingly, in this one, Blossom is zapped into the future—the 1980s. Many reviewers found this to be a letdown. However, in the fourth Blossom Culp book, *Blossom Culp and the Sleep of Death*, critics were happy to return to the past, and the book received critical acclaim. These books remain very popular with readers. Young people respond to Blossom because she is both unique and fearless.

CONFRONTING CONFORMITY

Many young people today are lonely or feel alienated from society. Peck believes that the suburban lifestyle has contributed to these feelings. He has very strong views on suburbs, where most of his audience comes from. He believes that suburbs thrive on conformity and often do not let in the outside world: "I had to learn on my own that a lot of people move to suburbs not to deal with life's problems, but to avoid them, that there are people who believe they deserve utopia because they paid so much for the house."[5]

Peck often writes about friendship and peer influence. In all of his books, Peck stresses the individual and encourages young adults to take responsibility and to stand up for themselves. His basic message is: "You will be held responsible for the consequences of your actions."[6] This message is portrayed in his second book, *Dreamland Lake*, about three 13-year-olds, Flip, Brian, and Elvan. Flip is the leader, but

Did you know...

One character who stands out from the crowd is Priscilla Roseberry from Peck's short story "Priscilla and the Wimps." Peck was working on a novel when an editor from a teen magazine called and asked him to write a short story. He said he had never written a short story before. She said they would pay him $300. She also told him that the story had to be very short, about 1,000 words, needed to end with a bang, and should be set in junior high or middle school. Also, she needed the story by that Thursday. Peck had 36 hours to write the story. He put away the novel he was working on, realizing that, for the next 36 hours, he would not be leaving the house and would be eating all of his meals at his desk. "Priscilla and the Wimps" became one of his most anthologized and well-known short stories.

Brian, more of a follower, is on the road to being able to think for himself. Though the novel is one of Peck's more serious, there is still humor throughout. Humor, Peck has discovered, is one of the best ways to connect with young readers.

RETURNING TO THE PAST

Peck's first four novels were set in contemporary times. When he wrote his fifth novel, *The Ghost Belonged to Me*, he felt like he needed a break from modern youth culture. The past came back to him—memories of his own childhood and the stories he had heard growing up. He wanted to pass on something of the past to today's children. He also wanted to show them that the world is a much bigger place—to teach them about times and places with which they may not be familiar. He explains, "I'm also moved to set my stories in past eras because I think this generation of young people is learning very little history and very little geography. I hope my novel can spark interest in history and geography." [7]

Peck set *The Ghost Belonged to Me* in the early 1900s in Bluff City, which was a recreation of his hometown. Written as a comedy and a ghost story, the novel features Alexander Armsworth, his Uncle Miles, and, of course, Blossom Culp. A New Orleans girl who died in the Civil War has been haunting the barn loft on Alexander's property for years. Only Uncle Miles remembers the real story about her.

Though the book is based on some of Peck's memories of his real Uncle Miles, Peck did not tell the story of his own childhood or use himself as a character. Instead, he wrote about some of the town's eccentric characters using stories he had heard as a child. He chose to tell the story about his hometown in the early twentieth century, as recalled by his great-uncle, Miles Peck.

Peck realized he could not depict Miles as he had been in life. For one thing, Peck cleaned up Miles's language. He also turned him into a bachelor in the novel, although in real life, he was married several times. The biggest change he made was to give Miles and the young great-nephew a close relationship with each other. In real life, Miles did not usually pay much attention to Peck.

Peck's own uncle never would have told ghost stories, either, but Peck wanted to include them for his readers. Fans had written him letters requesting that he write a ghost story, or something about "the weird." After writing a couple of novels, Peck realized he needed to write what the kids wanted to hear about. He states:

> I'd been trying to write responsible, reasonably realistic novels of modern life. I'd wanted to hold up a mirror to my readers. I'd thought they wanted to be recognized by books. They did, but they wanted to see themselves in more interesting (less seriously challenging) settings. They wanted characters that reminded them of themselves in fantasy.[8]

Earlier in his career, Peck would not have thought about writing stories about the supernatural, but now he saw that this was what kids wanted to read. It was also a fun way to write a story. When he was working on *The Ghost Belonged to Me*, the "minute this dead girl stepped on the stage, the story came alive."[9] Then he realized he also needed a living girl, to balance the ghost. Thus, the literary birth of Blossom Culp. Peck mixes humor and the supernatural, and, at the same time, teaches kids about the past. Through use of time-travel plot devices, readers can learn about the sinking of the *Titanic*, ancient Egypt, and the women's suffrage movement.

Since the publication of *The Ghost Belonged to Me*, many of Peck's other books have also taken place in the past and in small towns. Whether set in historical or contemporary times, Peck's work usually includes older characters, as well. "There's an elderly character in every one of my novels—for fear there aren't enough elders in the lives of my readers," he attests.[10] Today, many kids grow up without knowing their grandparents. The old are often hidden away in nursing homes, or families are split up, living far away from each other. Peck feels that one way young people can learn something about the past, and about the lives of their own grandparents, is to include elderly characters in his stories.

The elderly in Peck's books are oftentimes his most memorable characters. Uncle Miles Peck, Grandma Dowdel, and Granddad Fuller in *Fair Weather* are all vibrant, kooky, and strong characters. Peck explains his reason for including them:

> I need them. Young readers need them more. The old folks are there in the novels as counterbalances. They provide wisdom and seasoning won only through long lifetimes, and compassion unavailable from the peer group. They offer alternatives in the acceleration battle between parents and children, and glimpses of the problems and sorrows of old age for a young generation fixated on their own.[11]

Peck's older characters are usually a very positive influence on the young main character. For example, in *Those Summer Girls I Never Met*, Drew and his sister go on a summer cruise with their grandmother, who ends up being a much more interesting person than they ever imagined. Drew realizes he hardly knew his grandmother before then. Aunt Fay Moberly in *Strays Like Us* encourages Molly to stand up for herself. She is wise and caring. The old people in Peck's books are often eccentric and spunky, and provide a link to the past, such as the balding, gold-toothed Polly Prior, Kate's great-grandmother in one of Peck's earlier books, *Remembering the Good Times.* She is a wise, helpful woman in Trav's life, but she cannot imagine anyone as promising as him throwing his life away.

Where does Peck get his elderly characters? In addition to Uncle Miles, other people from Peck's past have also showed up in his fiction. For example, the life of his grandmother—though not her personality—inspired the character of Grandma Dowdel, one of his most beloved characters. Grandma Dowdel is the star of *A Long Way from Chicago* and *A Year Down Yonder.* Peck's own grandmother was the sole survivor of a smallpox epidemic. As an infant she was found alive, with two dead parents and a dead twin sister; she lived to be 93. In Peck's view, that is why Grandma Dowdel goes to live with Aunt Puss, though it is not a story he actually tells in the book. Peck describes Grandma Dowdel as a composite character, which means she is based on several people, as well as what he made up. He explains, "She is all of my great aunts, and while she is not much like my grandmother—except physically—all were imposing women. . . . It was a matriarchy, and Grandma Dowdel represents that."[12] Grandma Dowdel is feisty, independent, and, in Peck's view, "She was, in fact, my retort to all those cloying portrayals of sweet little old ladies knitting by the fire in kiddies' picture books."[13] He has also hinted that Grandma Dowdel is actually the grown-up version of Blossom Culp.

Peck likes to write about the past in order to reach the young, to let the old and young overlap. Many of Peck's stories are fun to read aloud, which can encourage adults and kids to spend time together. For example, *The Ghost Belonged to Me* was popular among teachers and librarians for the stories within stories that could easily be read aloud. In the *New York Times Book Review*, the reviewer, Jim Gladstone, says of *A Year Down Yonder*, "I suspect that parents and grandparents will enjoy reading these conversationally cadenced stories aloud."[14]

Peck's books—whether dramas or ghost stories—reach out to his audience in a real and believable way. The protagonist, always a young person, is someone the reader can identify with. Peck does not write books in which young people are the only characters, though. He brings in grandparents and great-grandparents to give the stories richness and, often, unpredictability.

Richard Peck believes that writing is neither a craft nor a job, but a "way of looking at the world."

6

How He Works

FOR RICHARD PECK, “Writing isn’t a job, it’s a way of looking at the world—so I have to write to see.”[1] Even when he’s not writing, Peck is thinking about writing.

Writers do not spend all their time sitting at a desk. They also must pay attention to the world around them to get ideas for characters, settings, and conflicts. Sometimes writers conduct research for their books. They work out ideas and find inspiration. They spend a great deal of time rewriting, editing, and shaping their work.

Peck does all of these things. He is very observant, especially when he travels to schools to talk with students. He is a good eavesdropper and a great listener. He turns many of the stories he hears into fiction—stories from when he was a kid and stories he hears now from teachers and students.

Peck also conducts extensive research for his work. Not only does he visit schools to talk with students, but he also reads, goes to libraries to do research, and collects important, useful information for his work. Over the years, he has accumulated thick files, filled with research, on the issues that have come up in novels, including rape, suicide, and shopping malls. He also researches historical time periods and admits, "In a way, it's easier to research the past than to nail the speech, the trends, the look of the present—and to wonder how long they'll last."[2]

For *Fair Weather*, his novel about the World's Fair in Chicago, Peck went to the Chicago Historical Society Museum and read many official records, along with newspapers and magazines, from 1893 in order to capture an accurate description of the time and place. Eventually, he realized he had to get to the actual writing:

> My research kept leading me in all these directions and one day I thought, how many directions can you go in one book? Do you think it's time to go home now and write? The day comes when you realize it's so much easier to research than to create, but since you are spinning your wheels, you go home and just write. Then when you need more information, you go back to the library.[3]

A writer also reads. Throughout his career, Peck has stressed that a person cannot be a writer without being a reader. Reading good books is often what leads a person to write, and reading is also one of the best ways to learn how to write. Peck read all the time as a kid and still has a book with him at all times. He says, "I never go out for a cup of coffee without taking a book with me. When I pack to travel, I pack the book and notebook before the clothes. I'm reading or writing all my conscious hours."[4]

Peck, as we know, travels across the country to meet with students. Spending time with students gives him ideas and allows him to be around his audience, so that his fiction is able to be a realistic representation of their lives. Peck does not write while he is on the road; instead, he gathers ideas for his fiction and soaks in everything he observes about young people—the music they listen to, the way they dress, the words they use. He wants to write about what is important to kids. He admits, "Now, I never start a novel until some young reader, somewhere, gives me the necessary nudge."[5]

Ideas come from many sources, though. Peck writes not only from what he sees but also from what he imagines. Peck answers the question "And How Do You Get Your Ideas?" in his book *Love and Death at the Mall*:

> From observation, not experience; from research, not autobiography. If Ernest Hemingway really had fought all those wars and bulls, if he really had climbed all those mountains and caught all those fish, if he really had loved all those women, he wouldn't have had the time to write, let alone the need. We get our ideas from memories, usually of other people, even other people's memories. And from other people's books. We're always looking to other people for our stories, then creating other people to tell them.[6]

A WRITER'S ROUTINE

Writers need inspiration, but they must also be disciplined and dedicated. Peck is dedicated to the craft of fiction

A true technophobe, Peck prefers to write on a Royal Standard typewriter, such as the one seen above, rather than a computer.

and follows a writing routine. He writes from his apartment on the Upper West Side of Manhattan. According to his biographer, Donald Gallo, on the days that Peck writes, before he gets started, he likes to go outside, take a walk around the block, and buy a cup of coffee. Then he goes back to his apartment, pretending he's arrived at his office. It is a habit he started many years ago. Sometimes, people do not realize how much work writing is—this routine helps get Peck in the right frame of mind so that he can do his job.

Many writers follow a strict writing schedule, in which they write at the same time every day. For example, they write first thing in the morning or for a set number of hours. Peck does not follow a strict daily schedule. It differs as to what time he writes each day. He is not much of a morning person and needs to warm up a little before he can get started. Most of his best writing occurs later in the day. He feels flexible about how many hours he writes per day. When Peck first starts a novel, it takes him a while to get moving. He might work a couple of hours on it each day in the beginning. Once he gets further into the story, he devotes more hours of his day to writing.

Peck's office in his apartment is plain, simple, and comfortable. It is furnished with a few antiques from the early 1900s. It is modest and neat. He is one of the few writers today who does not write on a computer. Peck is skeptical of technology and prefers the "old-fashioned" methods

Did you know...

In a collection of stories she was compiling titled *Birthday Surprises*, editor Johanna Hurwtiz wanted to explore the idea that a child receives a beautifully wrapped box with nothing in it. When asked to contribute, Peck decided to write a story about Blossom Culp, who was already one of his most popular characters. Written as a precursor to the series of Blossom Culp novels, the story dramatizes the first impression Blossom makes when she arrives in Bluff City.

of writing—he still writes all his novels and stories on a Royal Standard typewriter. He is a *technophobe* (he dislikes technology). For years, he used the voice of his friend Paula Danziger, a fellow young adult writer, on his answering machine.

GETTING HIS IDEAS, CREATING CHARACTERS

Peck usually begins his novels with a theme or an idea—perhaps something that he heard from a student on one of his trips. He approaches the story from a teacher's point of view. A teacher might wonder what the story is about. Why was it written? What can a student learn from it?

Many writers base characters on themselves. Though Peck has based some of his stories on what he heard when he was a kid, he stresses again and again that he does not write autobiographically. He explains that he learned early on that children do not want to hear his nostalgia of growing up in the 1950s. He states, "They'd heard all these tales from their parents, and they didn't believe them. The young themselves warned me well in advance that a novel had better never be the autobiography of the author. It had far better be the biography of the person the reader would like to be."[7] He writes stories from the past, or from stories he heard while growing up, but he does not write about his own childhood. He tries to base his young characters more on his readers, not himself. He explains, "I try to write about my readers. I hope I'm giving my characters some traits some of the readers have."[8]

Characterization is a major part of good fiction, and Peck spends a lot of time developing the characters. He usually has a cast of characters that covers several

A photo of East 72nd Street in New York City, where Peck lived for many years.

generations—young people, parents, teachers, and grandparents. He writes about families, even when they are broken. He explains the importance of creating adult characters in his books:

> I'm careful with my portrayals of adults: parents, grandparents, stepparents. In my books stepparents aren't going to be villainous, because the young are too likely to do that casting themselves. Parents aren't going to be perfect, but they aren't going to be stereotypes. They're going to be portrayed as whole human beings with their own needs.[9]

Peck has written about kids whose parents are wealthy, poor, supportive, or absent. No matter what kind of parents they are, Peck portrays them as complex beings, with strengths and flaws.

Peck explains that he is always putting himself in the shoes of his characters: "I have to play every part. That's part of the job. The way I do that is by removing myself from the story. In order to be all the characters, I can't be there myself."[10]

Peck usually writes in the first person, to capture the voice of a teenager. About half of Peck's novels have a female narrator or are from a female's point of view. His female characters tend to be insightful, independent, and smart. They are unafraid to stand up for their beliefs. For example, in his first novel, *Don't Look and It Won't Hurt,* Carol Patterson empowers herself by running away to bring home her troubled sister. It is Carol who holds the family together. Peck has no trouble writing female characters and believes it may actually be easier: "Women are more generous in discussing their emotions than men are. Women are more verbal about the things novels are about . . . emotional topics." [11]

Peck also likes writing dialogue. Dialogue is an excellent way to reveal character and conflict. It also brings readers right into a story—they can hear the characters and feel like they are a part of a scene. Peck's good listening skills help him write realistic, believable dialogue. He also eavesdrops on conversations all the time. He listens to people in shopping malls, on buses, and on trains. He always has a notebook with him. He wants his dialogue to sound natural and believable.

Setting is another important aspect of Peck's writing. He thinks that today's students are not learning enough about geography, so he often writes about a place in the past and sets the novel in a small, rural town. He explains that he writes many of his books in small towns because "that is the tradition that I came from. Small town and rural Midwest. And I don't want it to die. I am writing for kids in suburbs who don't know that time or that place."[12] In these books he will often use real family names and places in his work. For example, he used real town names in *A Long Way from Chicago* and *A Year Down Yonder*, which resulted in an invitation back to his father's hometown to help open the new grade school. Other times, his fiction takes place in suburbia, because that is where his readers often live and they can identity with that setting. Though he loves New York City, Peck rarely sets novels in the city, because he feels that the majority of his readers do not live in large cities.

After Peck has the theme, characters, and setting, he moves on to developing the plot, although this part of the process intimidates him.

Some writers write an entire draft before revising. They like to get everything down in a rush, without much editing. Peck does not work this way. He works slowly and carefully, writing scene by scene. He does not like to jump around. He writes the story in order. Once he has the first few chapters written, the rest usually moves a little faster. Peck typically gets his books' titles from certain lines in the manuscript, so he never has a title when he begins writing. He pays close attention to picking titles but often finds it a difficult process. Sometimes, when trying to pick the right title, he makes long lists. He admits, "I once submitted 24 titles [to the publishers] before they accepted one."[13]

Revision and rewriting are a crucial part of writing a book. Peck averages about six or seven drafts per book, though the earlier chapters are usually worked on the most. Sometimes, he will write the first chapter as many as 25 times, until he feels he has it right.

Peck does not like to show his work to anyone until he is finished. Occasionally, he will break this rule to show the book to a small group of students. He likes to get their reactions, and he wants to hear what they think will happen next.

When Peck finishes a book, he sends it to his editor. Even though he is now a very successful and well-respected author, he still gets nervous about submitting his work. He feels the same kinds of pressure he felt when he began to write. It is easy to doubt yourself—even when you're successful. Peck explains that "all those blank pages have to be filled, because writing is making something out of nothing. The success of your last book, making you fear you will start going downhill. It's very intimidating. Very few people would choose to live in this kind of isolation and do work this speculative, but then writers aren't most people."[14] Peck also knows that he puts as much time, hard work, and care as he can into his fiction—that he tries to make it the best he is capable of producing.

A photo of the author and critic Phyllis Schlafly, taken on July 31, 1996, in St. Louis. In her syndicated column, Schlafly criticized the supernatural elements of Peck's Blossom Culp novels.

7

Freedom of Speech

PECK RESPECTS AND enjoys the work of many of today's young adult authors. It is as if they are all on the same team—all in it together, trying to reach young people through the written word. One of the best and most influential young adult writers, Peck asserts, was Robert Cormier, author of *The Chocolate War* and many other important books. Peck felt that the world of young adult literature suffered a great loss with Cormier's death in November 2000.

The first book Peck recommends teachers assign their students is Robert Cormier's *The Chocolate War.* He also recommends M.E. Kerr's *Night Kites* and Chris Crutcher's *Running*

Loose. He is a fan of S.E. Hinton and thinks that *The Outsiders* helped pave the way for young adult literature. Other books he recommends are Will Hobb's *Downriver*, Jerry Spinelli's *Stargirl*, Alex Flinn's *Breathing Underwater*, Sarah Dessen's *Dreamland*, Patricia McCormick's *Cut*, Walter Dean Myers's *Monster*, and Sara Ryan's *Empress of the World*.

FIGHTING CENSORSHIP

It is Peck's hope that teachers and parents get these books and others into the hands of young adults. Unfortunately, he knows it is not always easy. Sometimes, in fact, a parent will make it very difficult. The parent may think the book is a bad influence and try to have it banned from his or her child's school. Peck feels very strongly about the freedom to read, and he believes that censorship and banning books will only hurt children. Books have the power to expand minds. In his book *Invitations to the World*, Peck provides a list of dos and don'ts for parents. Three of the seven tips include points on book banning. Peck states:

> Never worry about a book corrupting your child. . . . Worry if your children aren't getting ideas from books. If your children aren't reading, they're at the mercy of the standards and whims of their peer group, standards to which you have less access than to what appears in print.[1]

Peck also advises, "Never use a book as a scapegoat for your inability to control your children's television addiction, and never worry over the words in a book your children already knew before they could read or see regularly written on walls." He tells parents, "Never try to ban a book unless you want to help the author publicize it."[2]

Over the years, many books have been banned in schools across the country. These books include classics such as *The Adventures of Huckleberry Finn*, *The Grapes of Wrath*, *Watership Down*, *The Catcher in the Rye*, *Brave New World*, and *To Kill a Mockingbird*, among others. Why would parents or schools want to keep such notable books out of students' hands? Book banning and censorship are topics that Peck addresses in his books *Invitations to the World* and *Love and Death at the Mall.* He believes that most censorship stems from fear and lack of imagination, and he calls on teachers and librarians to stick together. Pecks believes, "Only the nonreader fears books."[3]

TACKLING TOUGH TOPICS

Peck's books have not stirred up as much controversy as those of some of his colleagues, though many of his books, such as *Are You in the House Alone?*, *Close Enough to Touch*, and *Remembering the Good Times*, deal with topics that can spark strong emotions. Peck continues to write about real and complex issues in his newer work, mixing drama and humor. For example, in *Strays Like Us*, 12-year-old Molly gets sent to live with her great-aunt, Fay Moberly, after her mother, a drug addict, is hospitalized. One of Molly's new friends is Will. She later finds out that Will's father is dying of AIDS and that Will's grandparents are hiding his father in their home because they are afraid of what people in town will say if they find out he has AIDS. Molly's aunt is the only one who knows, and that is because she takes care of him.

Peck got the idea for this novel after he visited a rural school. He was waiting in the library for the students to show up. He expected to see farm kids, but when the buses pulled up, he saw "black leather and rainbow hair, and bristling with hardware—just plain bristling, in fact."

> "Who are *they*?" I asked the librarian beside me.
>
> "They're children sent by their parents or the social worker back to extended family, mostly grandparents."
>
> "How many?" I asked, amazed.
>
> "Seventy percent of the school," she said. "But for them, we'd be closed now."[4]

When the librarian told him that usually the arrangement did not work, he knew he had an idea for his next novel.

Strays Like Us received many good reviews. A reviewer for *Booklist* wrote, "Peck is at his best in this wry, unsentimental story of three generations in small-town Missouri: Their roots, their failures, their loving kindness."[5] A critic

Did you know...

In his short-story collection *Past Perfect, Present Tense*, Peck lists five "Helpful Hints" for kids who want to write a short story. Each hint is followed by a short explanation. These are the five hints:

Hint #1: Nobody but a reader ever became a writer.
Hint #2: Know the markets for short stories.
Hint #3: The only writing is rewriting.
Hint #4: A story is only as strong as the voices telling it.
Hint #5: A story is a question about change.

for *Publishers Weekly* remarked, "Peck not only understands the fragile emotions of adolescents, he also knows what kind of characters will pique their interest."[6]

AIDS is a topic many schools do not want to address, but Peck felt it was important to show the reality of it, along with drug addiction, friendship, and coming of age, in his novel. It is important, in addressing serious subjects, not to preach or tell the audience what to think. The young adult books that address serious subjects the best allow the characters to tell the stories in their own way.

Though he has dealt with serious and timely subjects, Peck's books have not been extremely controversial. For one thing, Peck does not write explicitly about sex or drugs. He also rarely uses profanity in his books; he works hard to keep his language clean so that authorities do not keep his books out of kids' hands. However, several years ago, even Peck began to appear on book-banning lists—and because of Blossom Culp, of all people. Phyllis Schlafly, in her syndicated Copley News Service column, suggested that *Ghosts I Have Been* and *The Ghost Belonged to Me* "could lead children to believe that, in order to be an interesting person, one should try to contact the dead and seek acquaintances who do likewise."[7] However, the majority of reviewers saw the books as harmless, fun, and engaging. For example, a critic for *Kirkus Reviews* wrote, "This haunting is slapstick most of the time . . . [Peck] will keep his audience giggling and just a little frightened at the same time."[8] Peck defends the supernatural as a good way to reach his readers. Does he believe in ghosts? "Not really, and may I never see one. But what would the history of literature, of storytelling, be without ghosts?"[9]

Peck was once invited by a school librarian to speak to junior high students, and one of the mothers refused to

***Above, Peck signs books at his fiftieth class reunion at DePauw University. Peck is very critical of efforts to ban books. His research into the subject of censorship was published in* The Last Safe Place on Earth.**

allow her son to read one of Peck's books that was on the reading list. Despite her protest, Peck went to the school at the encouragement of the teachers and librarians. As far as he knows, his books are still on that school library's shelf.

Peck supports such controversial books as Sara Ryan's *Empress of the World* and Alex Sanchez's *Rainbow Boys*, and disagrees with those authorities who want to censor them because the books have gay characters. He feels that these books, among many others, reflect the reality of students' lives and are important for young people—so they can see they are not alone, and that there are adults out there who see them as complex, individual human beings. "Stories aren't real life," Peck explains. "They're comments upon real life, parallel universes of what might be if our ties were stronger and the world a more coherent place."[10] When Peck was a teenager, one thing he and his friends lacked were books about teenagers—the young adult book had not yet been born. He admits, "We could have used some company and better role models than our schoolmates."[11]

Peck deplores the actions of Parents Against Bad Books in Schools, an association that promotes the censoring of many books. Peck writes that, with the ongoing problem of censorship, he is "reminded again of how little progress we've made in humanity and tolerance in a time when the young have been free to create their own tribal rules while their defeated parents go sulking in search of scapegoats."[12]

Books can make a difference in children's lives. They can teach and challenge them, as well as inspire them to use their imaginations. Peck believes it is important that students understand what is at risk. He asks:

> Why do I feel it is important to impress upon young readers their right to freedom of speech? Because so many of them don't know that they have freedom of speech. I'm not sure their peer group leaders give them freedom of speech. And I do know that the school library of the school they attend is under heavier attack than the public library just down the street. I think they are in the thick of the battle and many of them are not aware of it.[13]

WRITING ABOUT CENSORSHIP

As Peck heard about more incidents of books being banned, he started to collect information. He filled file folders with newspapers and magazine articles on censorship and book banning. One day, he realized he would write about this: "I thought it was time to write a book asking the young themselves where they stood on the censorship wars."[14] Peck knew he was not alone. He felt support from the Right to Read programs and the celebration of banned books by the American Library Association (ALA) and many librarians. Since 1982, the ALA has sponsored "Banned Books Week: Celebrating the Freedom to Read," which is observed during the last week of September each year. This event reminds Americans not to take the precious democratic rights of free speech and intellectual freedom for granted. The week celebrates the freedom to choose and to express one's opinion, even if that opinion might be considered unpopular. The ALA stresses that books must be made available to all who wish to read them. In general, Peck feels a kinship with young adult librarians and holds great respect for them.

This idea and research about censorship led to Peck's book *The Last Safe Place on Earth.* Fifteen-year-old Todd develops a crush on Laura, his little sister's babysitter, but then discovers Laura is brainwashing his sister, making her afraid of even dressing up for Halloween. Laura is part of a sect of fundamentalist Christians who believe that Halloween is evil. As Todd's eyes open, he realizes that his town is filled with people who want to eliminate books from the high school, including Anne Frank's *The Diary of a Young Girl.* The place where he lives becomes terrifying.

Most of the reviews for *The Last Safe Place on Earth* were positive. A critic for *Booklist*, on the other hand, suggested the book was "a heavy-handed warning" but also believed that "Peck writes with wit and warmth that will sweep teens into a world they'll recognize."[15]

Peck continues to address the topic of censorship and book banning. It is hard enough to get kids to read today; they do not need books to be taken away from them. Otherwise, he believes, we as a society are in danger.

David Small (left)*, illustrator of* So You Want To Be President?*, and Richard Peck, author of* A Year Down Yonder*, pose for a photo on January 16, 2001, after winning the American Library Association's Randolph Caldecott and John Newbery medals—the most prestigious awards in children's literature.*

8

Critical Success

IN 1995, PECK'S colleague Harry Mazer wanted to put together a collection of gun stories to be called *Twelve Shots* and asked Peck for a contribution. Peck thought about it for a while. He guessed that most of the stories would be macho stories, about hunting or gangs on the streets, so he decided to submit something different. He wrote a comical story about a woman with a gun, called "Shotgun Cheatham's Last Night Above Ground," set in the early 1900s.

GRANDMA DOWDEL

His editor liked it and told him to expand that short story into an entire book. Peck liked the idea. He felt ready to write about the past again. He need a break from contemporary culture: "While my colleagues were coming up with a new range of rough, ready, and readable contemporary novels that rushed in where no parent dared to tread, I began to drift back."[1] "Shotgun Cheatham's Last Night Above Ground" became the first story in *A Long Way from Chicago*. Joey narrates the stories about Grandma Dowdel. He and his little sister, Mary Alice, live in Chicago, and in the summers they are sent to a rural town in Illinois to stay with their eccentric and adventurous grandmother. Peck describes Grandma Dowdel thus:

> She is the American tall tale in a Lane Bryant dress. There's more than a bit of Paul Bunyan about her, and even a touch of the Native American trickster tradition. And so is she multicultural? I'd like to think so. I never label her race, ethnicity, or origins, and heaven knows, she never tells. I'd like her to be the reader's grandmother, wherever in the wide world her village is.[2]

The book was a critical and popular success, and became the Newbery silver medalist in 1999.

After seeing the success of *A Long Way from Chicago*, Peck's editor suggested that he write a sequel. Peck was not sure. He had not planned on writing more stories about Grandma Dowdel. Besides, he felt like he was out of material because he had already included everything in the first book. He soon realized he could write a sequel if he had more stories. To remedy this, on Thanksgiving, he went home to Decatur and met up with his extended family, including distant cousins and people younger than himself. Peck gathered everyone around the Thanksgiving table and asked them to tell him stories. Stories about their parents, siblings, grandparents—everyone they knew. The stories soon flowed, one after another, many of them humorous. By the end of the visit, Peck felt like he had enough ideas to get started.

He also knew he needed to conduct more research so he could capture the setting and time period. In order to do this, Peck read every issue of *Time* magazine from 1937, beginning with January, and created a timeline for the entire year. He explained that these political and historical events would probably not show up in the book, but that it was important for him, the author, to know everything possible about the time period. Peck also looked through merchandise catalogs, including Lane Bryant and what his family used to call "Monkey Ward" (Montgomery Ward). Peck explained:

> These were very helpful because they tell you what things cost. You need so much information that isn't in the history books because people do not live in history books. Instead, they live in catalogues and magazines, newspapers, and radio, which was popular at that time, more so than now.[3]

Peck wondered how Joey could narrate any more stories, because Peck had ended *A Long Way from Chicago* with Joey leaving for the army. He then realized that Joey's sister, Mary Alice, who was older now, could be the narrator. In *A Year Down Yonder,* during the recession of 1937, 15-year-old Mary Alice is sent to live with Grandma Dowdel. *A Year Down Yonder* was another success, with both his young readers and critics.

THE NEWBERY MEDAL

Life continued on as normal for Peck. Then, one morning in 2001, his life changed. Peck recalls:

> I was lying in bed waiting for the alarm to go off, and I reached over and turned it off, but it kept ringing. It was the phone. I was innocent as could be until the final moment. The voice said, "This is Caroline S. Parr of the Newbery committee calling you from Midwinter ALA in Washington, DC. Your book, *A Year Down Yonder*, has won the Newbery Medal." And I said, "Would you repeat that?" So she said, "This is Caroline S. Parr . . ." and I said, "I got that part." Still I didn't believe it. I asked, "Would you tell me who the Honor Book winners are?" She listed the names, and none of them was mine. Then there was a cheer in the background and that was all. I sat there in complete silence. But I was also wide awake by then, so I shaved, got dressed, and an hour and a half passed of perfect silence. It was the last hour and a half of silence I have had since.[4]

Soon after the phone call, Peck's editor called to confirm the news, and within hours, he received calls from United Press International, Scripps Howard, and the *Boston Globe*. Later that day, National Public Radio called, and then the *Today* show with an invitation for an interview with host Katie Couric. It was not until that evening that Peck finally reached his mother with the news. She already knew, though—the local paper had just interviewed her.

Peck was not a stranger to critical success or awards. Before this honor, his books had been finalists for the Newbery and the National Book Award, and were chosen as ALA Notable Books and ALA Best Books for Young Adults. He received the Edgar Allan Poe Award from the Mystery Writers of America, along with several other awards and honors. Also, in 1990, he was chosen for the Margaret A. Edwards Award for his body of work.

Although all of these awards and honors were important to Peck, winning the Newbery gold medal in 2001 was like winning an Academy Award or a Pulitzer Prize. A prestigious and important award, the Newbery Medal was named for eighteenth-century British bookseller John Newbery. The Association for Library Service to Children, a division of the ALA, awards it each year to the author of the

Did you know...

In his nonfiction book *Invitations to the World*, Peck gives teachers ideas on how to approach teaching literature. He lists "Ten Questions to Ask About a Novel." These are good questions to think about when you are reading. The questions are:

1. **What would this story be like if the main character were of the opposite sex?**
2. **Why is this story set where it is (not *what* is the setting)?**
3. **If you were to film this story, what characters would you eliminate if you couldn't use them all?**
4. **Would you film this story in black and white or in color?**
5. **How is the main character different from you?**
6. **Why would or wouldn't this story make a good TV series?**
7. **What's one thing in this story that's happened to you?**
8. **Reread the first paragraph of Chapter 1. What's in it that makes you read on?**
9. **If you had to design a new cover of this book, what would it look like?**
10. **What does the title tell you about the book? Does it tell the truth?**

most distinguished contribution to American literature for children. The other books nominated in 2001 were *Hope Was Here* by Joan Bauer, *Because of Winn-Dixie* by Kate DiCamillo, *Joey Pigza Loses Control* by Jack Gantos, and *The Wanderer* by Sharon Creech.

Five months after Peck found out that he was the winner, he received the award at the Newbery-Caldecott award dinner in San Francisco. His mother, who was celebrating her ninety-fifth birthday the same week he received his Newbery Medal, joined him. In his acceptance speech, Peck was gracious, thanking his colleagues, supporters, and editors. He also took time to pay homage to his late colleague Robert Cormier, the renowned author of *The Chocolate War*.

After winning the Newbery, Peck received numerous phone calls and letters, offering him speaking engagements and asking him to grant interviews. He found himself very busy and missed his peaceful writing time. He also enjoyed traveling and meeting people, however. "When I was a kid I wanted to go everywhere and meet everybody, and now I do!" he admits.[5]

Since winning the Newbery, Peck has published several popular books, including *Fair Weather*. A short story called "The Electric Summer" was the inspiration for the novel; it was based on Peck's memory of his Aunt Geneva telling him about the time she went to the World's Fair and got a glimpse of the future. In the novel, 13-year-old Rose and her family travel from an Illinois farm to the World's Fair in Chicago in 1893. The World's Fair announced the future for America, with displays of electricity, movies, and mass media. Peck writes vividly of the dazzling lights and the excitement. Rosie says,

> Onward we went, and how can I explain how it was to us? There was no night. White electricity had lit the world and

A photo of the World's Columbian Exposition (also called the Chicago World's Fair), which was held in 1893. The exposition was the setting for one of Peck's recent popular novels, Fair Weather, *in which a young girl travels with her family from her Illinois farm to see the modern marvels of the age—including demonstrations of electricity and movies.*

> erased the stars. Now we were standing beside a long body of water, busy with drifting gondolas. On both sides of the pond stood the great pavilions of the Columbian Exposition, the White City. It was Greece and Rome again, and every column and curlicue lit by an incandescent bulb.[6]

Most reviews were very enthusiastic. "An engaging historical novel that will please a wider audience than the targeted age group," a *Booklist* reviewer remarked.[7] *Kirkus Reviews* was somewhat more low-key: "Not up to its promise, but good fun nonetheless."[8]

FACING A CHANGED WORLD

Fair Weather was published on September 10, 2001. The next day, the United States was attacked by terrorists who destroyed the World Trade Center in New York City and damaged the Pentagon outside of Washington, D.C. Peck felt jarred when he reread the opening line of his book: “It was the last day of our old lives, and we didn’t even know it.”[9]

After the terrorist attacks, Peck reiterated his belief in the need for rigorous education; schools need to focus on geography, history, and literacy. Students need to know that “the journey to the world begins in the library, not the gym.”[10] Peck feels it is important that children know history, because it often repeats itself. He also believes that schools should require a foreign language. If schools offered fewer electives and more in-depth traditional courses, Peck believes that students would be better equipped to face the world.

Peck feels that American attitudes about public education have resulted in a failed system. He is against the privatization of schools and believes in equality of education. He recognizes that the problems in schools today are much worse than when he was teaching. In Peck’s view, the parents who never show up to conferences, the students who care more about their images than their grades, the culture of violence, and the loneliness and isolation of many teens have all contributed to the decline of the education system.

This failure was shown tragically in a suburban high school in Littleton, Colorado, on April 20, 1999. At Columbine High School, two students shot to death 12 students and a teacher, and wounded 24 others before committing suicide. The massacre made headlines around the world, making Columbine a household name. Peck, like many teachers, writers, and parents, wondered: How can the students be reached?

Books are competing with iPods, video games, and cell phones for young people’s attention, he believes. Peck states, “The music, the electronics, the clothing industries continued to know just where to find this new generation, but their parents seemed not to know where to look, and some weren't looking."[11]

Peck continues to have hope that his books, and the books of his peers, will get into the hands of the students who need them most. He does not expect his books to provide teenagers with simple answers, but he does hope they will teach his audience something, as well as push them to think, question, and use their imaginations. He also hopes that his books will cross over from children to adult readers, to "open up a line of communication between the generations."[12]

In 2002, Peck published *Invitations to the World*, a nonfiction work that is an autobiography, a social commentary, and a writing manual, all rolled into one. This book, geared toward teachers and librarians, discusses the creative process and what young people read and why. In it, he encourages parents to read aloud to children even after they can read for themselves: "Books are bonds between you and them."[13] In addition to writing books for and about teens, Peck has published essays in *School Library Journal*, the *New York Times*, and *Parents* magazine, and he has also published book reviews in the *Los Angeles Times* and *American Libraries*.

WRITING FOR ADULTS

Peck does not write books only for teens; he has also written books for adults. Once, when he was on a book tour, a paperback publisher suggested he write a novel for adults. Peck said he could not. She wanted him to write a historical novel and asked him what he would write about. He said, if he were to write a historical novel for adults, he would write about the sinking of the *Titanic*. The editor said, "Give me 50 pages and an outline. I'll have the contract waiting in New York when we get home."[14] Peck spent several years writing *Amanda/Miranda*, a popular book for adult audiences. A fan of the book, a woman in her eighties, sent Peck her Pasadena mother's notes on the tragic story of the pioneer Oatman family. Peck used the notes and wove those events and historical figures into a new novel, also for adults, titled *This Family of Women.* He has also written poems and a children's book called *Monster Night at Grandma's House.*

Peck's works have been translated into several languages, and continue to be critical and popular successes. He says it is hard to pick his favorite among all the books he has written. "They are all my babies," he says. "I have to be proud of them all, because each book was the best I could do at that time."[15] However, he admits he is very proud of *A Year Down Yonder* for winning the Newbery Medal and thinks that one of his earlier books, *Remembering the Good Times*, may be his best one.

Peck feels happy with his career and grateful for his success. He says, "The first book I ever wrote is still in print. So I'm happy about that. . . . *A Year Down Yonder* won the Newbery Award. What is meaningful to me about those books is that they are 30 years apart, and how grateful I am to have a career like this that has gone on for so long."[16]

HIS RECENT BOOKS

In 2003, Peck published a serious novel dealing with race and slavery. *The River Between Us* is set during the early days of the Civil War. The Pruitt family, living in rural Illinois, takes in two mysterious young ladies who arrive on a steamboat from New Orleans. There is an air of mystery about them. One of the women has a darker skin complexion, and people guess that she is the slave of the other woman. Their arrival forever changes the lives of the Pruitts. Critics responded with positive reviews, with a reviewer from *Kirkus* describing it as a "rich tale full of magic, mystery, and surprise," and noting, "Peck's spare writing has never been more eloquent than in this powerful mystery in which personal secrets drive the plot and reveal the history."[17]

Peck has also published comic novels, including *The Teacher's Funeral: A Comedy in Three Parts* and *Here Lies the Librarian. The Teacher's Funeral: A Comedy in Three Parts* is set in rural Indiana in 1904. Fifteen-year-old Russell's dream of quitting school and joining a wheat threshing crew is thwarted when his older sister takes over the teaching at his one-room schoolhouse. Positive reviews cited Peck's humor and good dialogue. The historical setting also teaches readers about how modern technology was beginning to transform America with motorcars, telephones, and steel-threshing machines.

Here Lies the Librarian is also set in rural Indiana, in 1914. Four young librarians arrive in a small Indiana town, awakening the sleeping town. The protagonist is 14-year-old Eleanor "Peewee" McGrath, a tomboy and automobile enthusiast. The book received mostly positive reviews, though a reviewer for *Booklist* pointed out that "the pace lags, and the story is choppy."[18] However, the *School Library Journal* critic disagreed: "Another gem from Peck, with his signature combination of quirky character, poignancy, and outrageous farce."[19] Not only is this a coming-of-age story, but this humorous and fast-paced book also weaves in historical events, such as early feminism and the history of the automobile, and it serves as a tribute to the industrial and social revolutions.

Peck also published a collection of short stories called *Past Perfect, Present Tense: New and Collected Stories.* The collection gathers 11 of Peck's stories that were previously published in young adult anthologies and includes 2 new, previously unpublished ones. In addition to the stories, Peck includes notes about each—where the stories came from, and how and why he wrote them. He believes that, in order for a young adult story to be successful, the character must be left one step closer to maturity by the end; then readers will gain something important from the story. He also believes, "Like all novels, the young-adult novel has to entertain before it can do anything else."[20]

Peck is a versatile writer whose books represent many genres: mystery, history, contemporary realism, and ghost stories. Most notable are his coming-of-age novels that emphasize the importance of independence. Peck's novels often end without a neat conclusion—there are no easy answers. Peck has said often that fiction should not provide easy answers, but ask questions: "We write not what we know, but what we wonder about. A novel is about uncertainties."[21] He also likes to use humor in his work, even in serious novels. His work brings together the old and young to create rich, diverse stories.

A TEACHER STILL

Although Peck has not been a full-time teacher since 1971, for several years he signed on as a temporary lecturer on around-the-world cruises. This allowed him to travel, teach, and meet people who often provided inspiration for characters in his books. He has also been a guest teacher in many schools and has taught university courses on young adult literature. He is an adjunct professor with Louisiana State University's School of Library and Information Science. In 2001, Peck attended the first National Book Festival at the White House, along with writers Scott Turow, Walter Dean Myers, Patricia MacLachlan, and Jon Scieszka.

Though Peck quit teaching, in many ways he is still a teacher of the young. He admits:

> In a way, writing is an extension of teaching. Everything is. Teaching is a job you never quit. You just go on and on trying to turn a life into lesson plans. Every word I read and every word I write causes me to ask: How would I present that in class? Would they accept this? How would they see this? I write for mythical students, and when I go into classrooms, I get wonderful information, especially from the teachers and the librarians who are there on the firing line every day, and can tell me things that nobody else knows and that the kids dare not say.[22]

Peck did not know when he began that he would make a career out of writing, but he is committed to writing more books and to reaching out to young people with his novels. He has no plans to stop writing. When asked how much longer he will write, he answers:

> As long as the letters keep coming, providing grins and the occasional tear. As long as my colleagues keep writing books that I admire and learn from, and wish I'd written. As long as coming of age continues to be so much harder than anything I can remember. As long as I can eavesdrop on other people's lives and stick my nose into their personal business, and call it "research."[23]

Peck never expected to become a well-known novelist, but he did think that he would make a good teacher. Now, he is both—a widely read and well-respected young adult authors who continues to teach young people through his engaging stories and well-liked characters.

CHRONOLOGY

1934 Richard Peck is born April 5 in Decatur, Illinois, to Wayne and Virginia Peck.

1952 Enters DePauw University and plans to be a teacher.

1954 Sails to England on the *Ile de France* and spends junior year at Exeter University.

1956 Graduates from DePauw and enters the army; spends two years in Germany as a company clerk and a chaplain's assistant.

1958 Enters graduate school at Southern Illinois University at Carbondale; serves as a teaching assistant in the English department.

1961 Teaches English at Glenbrook North High School in Northbrook, Illinois.

1963 Works as a textbook editor for Scott, Foresman and Company in Chicago.

1965 Begins teaching English and education at Hunter College and Hunter College High School in New York City. Self-publishes *Old Town, A Complete Guide: Strolling, Shopping, Supping, Sipping* with Norman Strasma.

1966 Coedits *Edge of Awareness: Twenty-Five Contemporary Essays* with Ned E. Hoopes.

1969 Serves a yearlong fellowship in Washington, D.C., as assistant director of the Council for Basic Education.

1970 Edits *Sounds and Silences: Poetry for Now.*

1971 Edits *Mindscapes: Poems for the Real World*; resigns from teaching in order to write full time.

1972 His first novel, *Don't Look and It Won't Hurt*, is published.

1973 *Dreamland Lake* and *Through a Brief Darkness* are published.

1974 *Representing Super Doll* is published.

1975 *The Ghost Belonged to Me* is published.

1976 *Are You in the House Alone?* is published and wins the Edgar Allan Poe Award.

1977 *Ghosts I Have Been* and *Monster Night at Grandma's House*, illustrated by Don Freeman, are published; Peck is awarded Illinois Writer of the Year.

1978 *Father Figure* is published.

1979 *Secrets of the Shopping Mall* is published.

1980 *Amanda/Miranda*, his first adult novel, is published.

1981 *Close Enough to Touch* and *New York Time* are published.

1983 *The Dreadful Future of Blossom Culp* and *This Family of Women* are published.

1985 *Remembering the Good Times* is published.

1986 *Blossom Culp and the Sleep of Death* is published.

1987 *Princess Ashley* is published.

1988 *Those Summer Girls I Never Met* is published.

1989 *Voices After Midnight* is published.

1990 Peck wins the Margaret Edwards Young Adult Author Achievement Award and the National Council of Teachers of English/ALAN Award, for outstanding contributions to young adult literature.

1991 *Unfinished Portrait of Jessica* and *Anonymously Yours* are published.

1993 *Bel-Air Bambi and the Mall Rats* is published.

1994 *Love and Death at the Mall* is published.

1995 *The Last Safe Place on Earth* and *Lost in Cyberspace* are published.

1996 *The Great Interactive Dream Machine* is published.

1998 *London Holiday* and *Strays Like Us* are published.

1999 Younger version of *Amanda/Miranda* is published; *A Long Way from Chicago* is named a Newbery Honor book and National Book Award finalist.

2001 *Fair Weather* is published; *A Year Down Yonder* wins the Newbery Medal; Peck is presented with the National Humanities Medal for lifetime achievement; *Invitations to the World: Teaching and Writing for Young* is published.

2003 *The River Between Us* is published.

2004 *Past Perfect, Present Tense: New and Collected Stories* and *The Teacher's Funeral: A Comedy in Three Parts* are published; *The River Between Us* is awarded the Scott O'Dell Award for Historical Fiction.

2006 *Here Lies the Librarian* is published.

2007 *On the Wings of Heroes* is published.

NOTES

Chapter 1

1 Richard Peck, *Love and Death in the Mall.* New York: Delacorte, 1994, p. 34.

2 Donald R. Gallo, *Presenting Richard Peck*. Boston: Twayne, 1989, p. 2.

3 Richard Peck, *Anonymously Yours.* Englewood Cliffs, N.J.: Julian Messner, 1991, pp. 64–65.

4 Peck, *Love and Death in the Mall*, p. 61.

5 "Richard Peck Interview," Scholastic: Authors and Books. http://books.scholastic.com/teachers/authorsandbooks/authorstudies/authorhome.jsp?authorID=5557&&displayName=Interview%20Transcript.

6 Peck, *Love and Death at the Mall*, p. 82.

Chapter 2

1 *Peck, Love and Death at the Mall*, p. 10.

2 Nancy J. Johnson and Cyndi Giorgis, "Newbery Interview: A Conversation with Richard Peck," *Reading Teacher,* 4 (Dec. 2001–Jan. 2002): pp. 392–397.

3 Peck, *Anonymously Yours*, p. 20.

4 Ibid., p. 19.

5 Peck, *Love and Death at the Mall*, p. 11.

6 Ibid., p. 6.

7 Ibid., p. 4.

8 Ibid., p. 5.

9 Ibid., p. 3.

10 Ibid.

11 Peck, *Anonymously Yours*, p. 81.

12 Ibid., p. 62.

13 Ibid., p. 79.

14 Ibid., p. 82.

Chapter 3

1 Peck, *Love and Death at the Mall*, p. 48.

2 Ibid., p. 45.

3 Ibid., p. 52.

4 Ibid., p. 53.

5 Ibid., p. 57.

6 Ibid., p. 60.

7 Ibid., p. 68.

Chapter 4

1 Gallo, *Presenting Richard Peck*, p. 18.

2 Richard Peck, *Strays Like Us*. New York: Dial Books, 1998, p. 16.

3 Peck, *Love and Death at the Mall,* p. 85.

4 Peck, *Anonymously Yours*, p. 6.

5 Ibid., p. 104.

6 Gallo, *Presenting Richard Peck,* p. 32.

7 "Richard Peck Interview," Scholastic: Authors and Books.

http://books.scholastic.com/teachers/authorsandbooks/authorstudies/authorhome.jsp?authorID=5557&&displayName=Interview%20Transcript.

8 Peck, *Love and Death at the Mall*, p. 128.

9 "Newbery-Winning Richard Peck," Tallmania. http://www.tallmania.com/peck.html.

10 Peck, *Love and Death at the Mall*, p. 29.

11 Ibid., p. 96.

12 Ibid., p. 98.

13 Johnson and Giorgis, "Newbery Interview: A Conversation with Richard Peck," pp. 392–397.

14 Peck, *Love and Death at the Mall*, p. 113.

15 Ibid.

16 Peck, *Anonymously Yours*, p. 47.

17 Peck, *Love and Death at the Mall*, p. 114.

18 Ibid., p. 42.

Chapter 5

1 Peck, *Love and Death at the Mall*, p. 28.

2 Ibid., p. 81.

3 Ibid., p. 75.

4 Ibid., p. 76.

5 Ibid., p. 36.

6 Ibid., p. 106.

7 "Richard Peck Interview," Scholastic: Authors and Books. http://books.scholastic.com/teachers/authorsandbooks/authorstudies/authorhome.jsp?authorID=5557&&displayName=Interview%20Transcript.

8 Peck, *Love and Death at the Mall*, p. 14.

9 Richard Peck, *Past Perfect, Present Tense: New and Collected Stories.* New York: Dial Books, 2004, p. 69.

10 Ibid., p. 113.

11 Peck, *Love and Death at the Mall*, p. 20.

12 Johnson and Giorgis, "Newbery Interview: A Conversation with Richard Peck," pp. 392–397.

13 Richard Peck, *Invitations to the World.* New York: Dial Books, 2002, p. 185.

14 Jim Gladstone, "Bright Lights, Big City," *New York Times Book Review*, March 11, 2001, p. 27.

Chapter 6

1 "Richard Peck Interview," Scholastic: Authors and Books. http://books.scholastic.com/teachers/authorsandbooks/authorstudies/authorhome.jsp?authorID=5557&&displayName=Interview%20Transcript.

2 Peck, *Invitations to the World,* p. 183.

3 Johnson and Giorgis, "Newbery Interview: A Conversation with Richard Peck," pp. 392–397.

4 "Richard Peck Interview," Scholastic: Authors and Books. http://books.scholastic.com/teachers/authorsandbooks/authorstudies/authorhome.jsp?authorID=5557&&displayName=Interview%20Transcript.

5 "Newbery-Winning Richard Peck," Tallmania. http://www.tallmania.com/peck.html.

6 Peck, *Love and Death at the Mall*, p. 65.

7 Ibid., p. 10.

8 "Richard Peck Interview," Scholastic: Authors and Books. http://books.scholastic.com/teachers/authorsandbooks/authorstudies/authorhome.jsp?authorID=5557&&displayName=Interview%20Transcript.

9 Peck, *Love and Death at the Mall*, p. 138.

10 "Richard Peck Interview," Scholastic: Authors and Books. http://books.scholastic.com/teachers/authorsandbooks/authorstudies/authorhome.jsp?authorID=5557&&displayName=Interview%20Transcript.

11 Ibid.

12 Johnson and Giorgis, "Newbery Interview: A Conversation with Richard Peck," pp. 392–397.

13 Ibid.

14 "Richard Peck Interview," Scholastic: Authors and Books. http://books.scholastic.com/teachers/authorsandbooks/authorstudies/authorhome.jsp?authorID=5557&&displayName=Interview%20Transcript.

Chapter 7

1 Peck, *Invitations to the World,* p. 198.

2 Ibid.

3 Peck, *Love and Death at the Mall*, p. 144.

4 Peck, *Invitations to the World,* p. 182.

5 "Strays Like Us," *Booklist*, Vol. 94, no. 15 (April 1, 1998): p. 1325(1).

6 "Strays Like Us," *Publishers Weekly* Vol. 245, no. 15 (April 13, 1998): p. 76.

7 Peck, quoted in *Love and Death at the Mall*, p. 143.

8 "The Ghost Belonged to Me," *Kirkus Reviews*, April 1, 1975.

9 Peck, *Past Perfect, Present Tense: New and Collected Stories,* p. 68.

10 Peck, *Love and Death at the Mall,* p. 14.

11 Peck, *Anonymously Yours*, p. 41.

12 Peck, *Invitations to the World,* p. 180.

13 "Newbery-Winning Richard Peck," Tallmania. http://www.tallmania.com/peck.html.

14 Peck, *Invitations to the World*, p. 156.

15 "The Last Place on Earth," *Booklist* Vol. 91, no. 10 (Jan. 15, 1995): p. 913(1).

Chapter 8

1 Peck, *Invitations to the World*, p. 183.

2 Ibid., p. 188.

3 Johnson and Giorgis, "Newbery Interview: A Conversation with Richard Peck," pp. 392–397.

4 Ibid.

5 "Richard Peck Interview," Scholastic: Authors and Books. http://books.scholastic.com/teachers/authorsandbooks/authorstudies/authorhome.jsp?authorID=5557&&displayName=Interview%20Transcript.

6 Richard Peck, *Fair Weather*. New York: Dial Books, 2001, pp. 62–63.

7 "Fair Weather," *Booklist* Vol. 98, no. 1 (Sept. 1, 2001): p. 110.

8 "Fair Weather," *Kirkus Reviews* Vol. 69, no. 14 (July 15, 2001): p. 1032.

9 Peck, *Fair Weather,* p. 1.

10 Peck, *Invitations to the World*, p. 192.

11 Ibid., p. 171.

12 Ibid., p. 189.

13 Ibid., p. 199.

14 Peck, *Love and Death in the Mall*, p. 115.

15 "Richard Peck Interview," Scholastic: Authors and Books. http://books.scholastic.com/teachers/authorsandbooks/authorstudies/authorhome.jsp?authorID=5557&&displayName=Interview%20Transcript.

16 Ibid.

17 "The River Between Us," *Kirkus Reviews* Vol. 71, no. 16 (August 15, 2003): p. 1077(1).

18 "Here Lies the Librarian," *Booklist* Vol. 102, no. 13, (March 1, 2006): p. 91.

19 "Here Lies the Librarian." *School Library Journal* Vol. 52, no. 4 (April 1, 2006): p. 146.

20 Peck, *Love and Death in the Mall*, p. 158.

21 Ibid., p. 101.

22 Johnson and Giorgis, "Newbery Interview: A Conversation with Richard Peck," pp. 392–397.

23 Peck, *Invitations to the World*, p. 173.

WORKS BY RICHARD PECK

1971 *Mindscapes: Poems for the Real World*

1972 *Don't Look and It Won't Hurt*

1973 *Dreamland Lake*; *Through a Brief Darkness*

1974 *Representing Super Doll*

1975 *The Ghost Belonged to Me*

1976 *Are You in the House Alone?*

1977 *Ghosts I Have Been*; *Monster Night at Grandma's House*

1978 *Father Figure*

1979 *Secrets of the Shopping Mall*

1981 *Close Enough to Touch*; *New York Time*

1983 *The Dreadful Future of Blossom Culp*; *This Family of Women*

1985 *Remembering the Good Times*

1986 *Blossom Culp and the Sleep of Death*

1987 *Princess Ashley*

1988 *Those Summer Girls I Never Met*

1989 *Voices After Midnight*

1991 *Unfinished Portrait of Jessica*; *Anonymously Yours*

1993 *Bel-Air Bambi and the Mall Rats*

1994 *Love and Death at the Mall: Teaching and Writing for the Literate Young*

1995 *The Last Safe Place on Earth*; *Lost in Cyberspace*

1996 *The Great Interactive Dream Machine*

1998 *London Holiday*; *Strays Like Us*; *A Long Way from Chicago*

1999 *Amanda/Miranda*; *A Year Down Yonder*

2001 *Fair Weather*; *Invitations to the World: Teaching and Writing for the Young*

2003 *The River Between Us*

2004 *The Teacher's Funeral: A Comedy in Three Parts*; *Past Perfect, Present Tense: New and Collected Stories*

2006 *Here Lies the Librarian*

2006 *On the Wings of Heroes*

POPULAR BOOKS

ARE YOU IN THE HOUSE ALONE?

High school junior Gail Osborn receives obscene and threatening notes and phone calls. She feels alone and does not know where to turn for help. Her feelings of isolation increase after she is raped by a boy she knows from school. Peck creates a sympathetic, insightful portrayal of one girl's survival through this terrible nightmare. Winner of the Edgar Allan Poe Award in 1976, this novel remains one of Peck's most widely read.

BLOSSOM CULP AND THE SLEEP OF DEATH

The fourth novel in the "Blossom Culp" series returns readers to Bluff City in 1914. The spirit of an ancient Egyptian princess contacts Blossom, who is gifted with "second sight." Blossom and Alexander are then catapulted into ancient Egypt, where they must help the princess—who has been dead for 3,500 years—regain her tomb. They also save a feminist schoolteacher from losing her job in 1914.

CLOSE ENOUGH TO TOUCH

Matt tells Dory he loves her, but soon afterward, she dies. Now Matt must deal with his grief and mourning. With this book—a tragic love story told from the boy's perspective—Peck wanted to write about a male character capable of expressing his feelings.

DON'T LOOK AND IT WON'T HURT

Peck's first novel, which he began writing the day he quit his teaching job. Fifteen-year-old Carol Patterson's father left when she was six, and her mother works most evenings as a hostess in a restaurant. When Carol's older sister, Ellen, becomes pregnant by a man currently serving a drug sentence, it is Carol who tries to hold the family together.

DREAMLAND LAKE

Best friends Flip and Brian find their lives changed forever after they discover a man dead near Dreamland Lake. The boys convince themselves that Elvan, a pitiful fat boy who has been trying to interest them in his collection of Nazi souvenirs, knows something about the man's death. The boys' adventure leads them on the path to a real tragedy.

FAIR WEATHER

Adventures abound when Lottie, Rosie, and Buster Beckett, accompanied by their eccentric granddad, leave the farm and head to the Chicago World's Fair in 1893. Peck describes the dazzling surprises the family encounters at the fair, such as riding a Ferris wheel and observing the skyscrapers and electrical lights. Some of the era's most famous real people, including Buffalo Bill, also appear.

THE GHOST BELONGED TO ME

This is the first book in the "Blossom Culp" series. Set in 1913 in Bluff City, Illinois, the ghost of a drowned girl haunts the Armsworth barn and warns Alexander of an impending disaster. It is Blossom Culp, the girl living next door to Alexander, though, who becomes the real star of the novel. Eccentric Uncle Miles also plays a part, helping the kids return the drowned girl's bones to her hometown of New Orleans.

GHOSTS I HAVE BEEN

In the second book of the series, Blossom Culp becomes involved with the ghost of a child who drowned on the *Titanic*. Blossom attempts to change history by rescuing the boy. Using her telepathic powers, she journeys to the doomed ship and to Queen Mary in Buckingham Palace.

HERE LIES THE LIBRARIAN

In 1914, four young librarians, all wealthy sorority sisters, arrive in a small Indiana town to reopen the town library. Meanwhile, 14-year-old Eleanor "Peewee" McGrath helps her brother run a garage and build his racecar. Peck conveys rural life in the early years of the twentieth century, weaving in early feminism and the history of the automobile.

THE LAST SAFE PLACE ON EARTH

In this novel about the dangers of book banning and censorship, 15-year-old Todd sees his perfect suburban world unravel when he discovers that Laura, the girl he has a crush on, is also a fundamentalist Christian who is brainwashing Todd's little sister. He begins to notice the many signs of censorship in his community and realizes the importance of looking beyond the carefully constructed facades.

A LONG WAY FROM CHICAGO: A NOVEL IN STORIES

Each summer over the nine years of the Depression, Joey and his sister, Mary Alice, leave Chicago to visit Grandma Dowdel in her rural Illinois town. In this collection of stories, Grandma Dowdel is continually surprising readers with her mischief, such as stealing the sheriff's boat or throwing cherry bombs.

REMEMBERING THE GOOD TIMES

One of Peck's most widely read books, this moving novel deals with teen suicide. Freshmen Trav, Kate, and Buck are good friends, but their friendship is not enough to save Trav. Learning how to grieve and how to accept help from adults is the focus of this poignant novel.

THE RIVER BETWEEN US

During the early days of the Civil War, the Pruitt family of Illinois takes in two mysterious young ladies who have fled New Orleans to come north. Is the darker-complexioned woman the other woman's slave? Personal secrets drive the plot. The novel depicts the truths about racism, war, and American history.

SECRETS OF THE SHOPPING MALL

With only four dollars between them, Teresa and Barnie hop a bus and ride to the end of the line, Paradise Park, which turns out to be a cement-covered suburban shopping mall. With no money and no place to go, they decide to stay. Barnie and Teresa spend their days and nights in a large department store. Just when they think they can live there unnoticed forever, they find out they are not alone.

STRAYS LIKE US

After her mother, a drug addict, is hospitalized, Molly finds herself living with her great-aunt Fay. Molly befriends their next-door neighbor, Will, a stray like herself. Aunt Fay, a nurse who treats patients in their homes, spends a lot of time next door because Will's father is dying of AIDS, although the family tries to cover this up.

THE TEACHER'S FUNERAL: A COMEDY IN THREE PARTS

Set in rural Indiana in 1904, 15-year-old Russell hopes to quit school and join a wheat threshing crew until his older sister takes over the teaching at his one-room schoolhouse after mean old Miss Myrt Arbuckle dies. This humorous novel depicts big-sister Tansy transforming the students, as modern technology transforms America with telephones and motorcars.

A YEAR DOWN YONDER

During the "Roosevelt Recession" in 1937, Mary Alice must leave Chicago and spend the year in a rural town with her feisty Grandma

Dowdel. After participating in many outrageous schemes, Mary Alice eventually learns to appreciate her grandmother's wisdom and her ways. This Newbery Medal winner is the sequel to *A Long Way from Chicago.*

POPULAR CHARACTERS

ALEXANDER ARMSWORTH

He is the original protagonist of the Blossom Culp books, telling his story in *The Ghost Belonged to Me.* Alexander, unlike Blossom, is from an affluent family. He is a good-looking boy who is sweetly naïve. He becomes friends with Blossom Culp, who tells him that he has second sight. He realizes this when he sees, and eventually talks to, the ghost of a young girl. In the books that follow *The Ghost Belonged to Me*, Alexander becomes Blossom's sidekick.

AUNT FAY MOBERLY

The aunt in *Strays Like Us*, Fay works all over town as a home nurse. She takes in her great-niece, Molly, when Molly's mother, a drug addict, is hospitalized. Aunt Fay is a hard worker and a strong woman. She is the one who takes care of Will's father, who is dying of AIDS. Peck has described Aunt Fay Moberly as a much more low-key version of Grandma Dowdel.

BLOSSOM CULP

Starting out as a secondary character in *The Ghost Belonged to Me*, Blossom becomes the star of the next three books in the series. Blossom is unpopular, unattractive, and from the wrong side of the tracks. Her alcoholic father left town, and her mother is a witch. Blossom is one of Peck's most popular characters. She is adventuresome, resourceful, and independent. Blossom also has telepathic powers and can time-travel. She takes Alexander with her on her adventures, journeying to the *Titanic* and ancient Egypt.

CAROL PATTERSON

The 15-year-old narrator of *Don't Look and It Won't Hurt*, Carol is the middle child in a family of three girls headed by a single mother who works constantly in order to make ends meet. Carol longs for a life that is not so ordinary. She is responsible and strong. She helps her mother take care of her younger sister, Liz. When her older sister, Ellen, gets pregnant and moves into a home for unwed mothers, Carol knows she must hold the family together.

ELEANOR "PEEWEE" MCGRATH

The teenage tomboy in *Here Lies the Librarian*, Peewee loves automobiles and her big brother, Jake. She is stubborn, fearless, and loyal. She and Jake run a struggling garage, where Jake is building a racecar. Peewee is spunky and adventurous. She is transformed by the arrival of four young librarians who teach her much about life.

GRANDMA DOWDEL

The star of *A Long Way from Chicago* and *A Year Down Yonder*, Grandma Dowdel is eccentric, rough, and gruff. She is a large woman who wears long dresses. She has developed a reputation in her small town, and many people are afraid of her. She can shoot a gun and she will twist the truth if necessary. At first, her grandchildren, Mary Alice and Joey, do not know what to make of her and worry that she is a bad influence. As time goes on, however, they realize that underneath the rough exterior is a loving person. Grandma Dowdel leads them on many unforgettable adventures. She outwits the banker, sets illegal fish traps, catches the town's poker-playing businessmen in their underwear, and saves the town from the terror of the Cowgill boys.

JIM ATWATER

As the protagonist of *Father Figure*, Jim is forced to grow up in a hurry. When his father leaves the family when Jim is young, Jim tries to be a father figure for his younger brother. After their mother commits suicide, Jim feels many emotions, including anger and betrayal. He and his brother are reunited with their father and move to Florida. Jim matures while he is there, gets to know his father, and deals with his tough emotions.

MARY ALICE

The narrator of *A Year Down Yonder* dreads leaving Chicago to go live in her grandmother's "hick town." This time her brother, Joey, who used to go with her during the summers (*A Long Way from Chicago*), will not be there. Mary Alice is a city girl and does not think she will survive in a place that does not even have a movie theater. She arrives with her cat, Bootsie, and a radio, wishing she were back home. Before long, though, she is an accomplice to Grandma Dowdel's schemes, and, by the end of the year, she has a hard time saying good-bye.

MATT MORAN

He is the protagonist of one of Peck's early novels, *Close Enough to Touch*. He falls in love with Dory, but then a tragedy occurs. The book focuses on how Matt deals with Dory's sudden death. He must go to her funeral and continue his life without her. Matt's pain and grief threaten to overwhelm him, but he faces his emotions and learns to love again.

ROSIE BECKETT

Thirteen-year-old Rosie is the narrator of *Fair Weather*. She is a hard worker on her parents' farm and is not afraid of killing a snake or skinning an animal. She is a steady, responsible girl. When she and her brother, sister, and granddad get the chance to go the World's Columbian Exposition in Chicago, Rosie is in awe of the spectacle. The fair inspires her to learn more about the world.

TANSY

Tansy is Lloyd and Russell's older sister in *The Teacher's Funeral.* The boys are dismayed to find out that Tansy will soon be their new teacher. She is hired to replace old Miss Myrt Arbuckle. Tansy is bossy, big, and teaches with vigor. She survives all of the boys' antics. Tansy has high expectations, but she is also a good teacher who does not give up on her students or her brothers.

UNCLE MILES

One of Peck's most memorable characters is Alexander Armsworth's uncle in *The Ghost Belonged to Me*. Uncle Miles swears, chews tobacco, and always speaks the truth. Miles knows the whole story about the death of Inez Dumaine, the girl who is now haunting the Armsworths' barn. He is truthful and loyal, and does not care about the niceties of life.

MAJOR AWARDS

1974 *Representing Super Doll* is named an ALA Book of the Year.

1976 *Are You in the House Alone?* wins the Edgar Allan Poe Award for best juvenile mystery novel and is named an ALA Book of the Year and one of *School Library Journal*'s Best Books of the Year.

1977 Peck awarded Illinois Writer of the Year by the Illinois Association of Teachers of English; *Ghosts I Have Been* is named an ALA Book of the Year, a *School Library Journal* Best Books of the Year, and a *New York Times* Outstanding Book of the Year.

1981 *Close Enough to Touch* is named an ALA Best Book for Young Adults and a *School Library Journal* Best Book for Young Adults.

1985 *Remembering the Good Times* is named a *School Library Journal* Best Book of the Year and an ALA Best Book for Young Adults.

1986 *Blossom Culp and the Sleep of Death* is named Child Study Association of America Children's Book of the Year.

1987 *Princess Ashley* is named an ALA Best Book for Young Adults.

1990 Peck wins the Margaret Edwards Young Adult Author Achievement Award and the National Council of Teachers of English/ALAN Award for outstanding contributions to young adult literature.

1991 Peck is awarded the Medallion from the University of Southern Mississippi, which honors authors who have made an outstanding contribution to the field of literature.

1997 Peck receives the Empire State Award, given by the New York Library Association's Youth Services section, for his body of work.

1999 *A Long Way from Chicago* is named a Newbery Honor Book and National Book Award finalist.

2001 *A Year Down Yonder* wins the Newbery Medal from the ALA; Peck is given the National Humanities Medal for lifetime achievement.

2003 *The River Between Us* is nominated for the National Book Award for young people's literature.

2004 *The River Between Us* is awarded the Scott O'Dell Award for Historical Fiction.

BIBLIOGRAPHY

Books

Gallo, Donald R. *Presenting Richard Peck.* Boston: Twayne, 1989.

Peck, Richard. *Anonymously Yours.* Englewood Cliffs, N.J.: Julian Messner, 1991.

———. *Fair Weather.* New York: Dial Books, 2001.

———. *Invitations to the World.* New York: Dial Books, 2002.

———. *Love and Death at the Mall.* New York: Delacorte Press, 1994.

———. *Past Perfect, Present Tense: New and Collected Stories.* New York: Dial Books, 2004.

———. *Strays Like Us.* New York: Dial Books, 1998.

Periodicals

"Fair Weather." *Booklist* Vol. 98, no. 1 (Sept. 1, 2001): p. 110.

"Fair Weather." *Kirkus Reviews* Vol. 69, no. 14 (July 15, 2001): p. 1032.

Gladstone, Jim. "Bright Lights, Big City." *New York Times Book Review,* March 11, 2001, p. 27.

"Here Lies the Librarian." *Booklist* Vol. 102, no. 13 (March 1, 2006): p. 91.

"Here Lies the Librarian." *School Library Journal* Vol. 52, no. 4 (April 1, 2006): p. 146.

Johnson, Nancy J., and Cyndi Giorgis. "Newbery Interview: A Conversation with Richard Peck." *Reading Teacher* 4 (Dec. 2001–Jan. 2002): pp. 392–397.

"The Last Place on Earth." *Booklist* Vol. 91, no. 10 (Jan. 15, 1995): p. 913(1).

"The River Between Us." *Kirkus Reviews* Vol. 71, no. 16 (August 15, 2003): p. 1077(1).

"Strays Like Us." *Booklist* Vol. 94, no. 15 (April 1, 1998): p. 1325(1).

"Strays Like Us." *Publishers Weekly* Vol. 245, no. 15 (April 13, 1998): p. 76.

Other Sources

"Newbery-winning Richard Peck," Tallmania. http://www.tallmania.com/peck.html.

"Richard Peck Interview," Scholastic: Authors and Books. http://books.scholastic.com/teachers/authorsandbooks/authorstudies/authorhome.jsp?authorID=5557&&displayName=Interview%20Transcript.

FURTHER READING

Collier, Laurie, and Joyce Nakamura, eds. *Major Authors and Illustrators for Children and Young Adults.* Farmington Hills, Mich.: Thomson Gale, 1993.

Gallo, Donald R., ed. *Sixteen: Short Stories by Outstanding Young-Adult Writers.* New York: Delacorte, 1984.

Mazer, Harry, ed. *Twelve Shots: Outstanding Short Stories About Guns.* New York: Delacorte, 1997.

Silvey, Anita, ed. *Children's Books and Their Creators.* New York: Houghton Mifflin, 1995.

Web Sites

Penguin Group—About Richard Peck
http://us.penguingroup.com/nf/Author/AuthorPage/0,,1000025091,00.html

Carol Hurst's Children's Literature Site
http://www.carolhurst.com/authors/rpeck.html

PICTURE CREDITS

page:

10: Pablo Martinez Monsivais/AP Images

20: © Bettmann/Corbis

29: Courtesy of DePauw University

32: Sarah A. Bonner/Spring Mount Photography

35: David Fenton/Getty Images

42: Library of Congress

51: Graham Wood/Getty Images

54: Library of Congress

64: Photo by Sonya Sones

68: Chaloner Woods/Getty Images

71: Sarah A. Bonner/Spring Mount Photography

76: James A. Finley/AP Images

82: Courtesy of DePauw University

86: Stuart Ramson/AP Images

93: Library of Congress, 6a27052

INDEX

ABOUT THE CONTRIBUTOR

AMY SICKELS received her MFA from Pennsylvania State University and has published stories and essays in literary journals such as the *Greensboro Review* and the *Madison Review*. She lives in New York City.